EXPERT PROFILES
VOLUME 17

Conversations with Influencers & Innovators

EXPERT PROFILES
VOLUME 17

Conversations with Influencers & Innovators

Featuring Conversations with

David Abrahams

Francisco Bermudez Jr

Marco Flores

Sally Gimon

Regina Gulbinas

L. Paul Hood, Jr

Donovan Manley

Lynda J. Roth

Jaime Sepulveda

Shannon Simmons

Sofiya Stasiv

Royalties from the Retail Sales of "Expert Profiles"
are donated to Global Autism Project

AUTISM KNOWS NO BORDERS;
FORTUNATELY NEITHER DO WE.®

Global Autism Project 501(c)3 is a nonprofit organization that provides training to local individuals in evidence-based practices for individuals with autism.

Global Autism Project believes that every child has the ability to learn and their potential should not be limited by geographical bounds.

The Global Autism Project seeks to eliminate the disparity in service provision seen around the world by providing high-quality training to individuals providing services in their local community. This training is made sustainable through regular training trips and contiguous remote training.

You can learn more about Global Autism Project by visiting GlobalAutismProject.org.

Table of Contents

Real Estate with Character

After dedicating years to serving in the Army and developing my leadership, planning, advising, and high-risk operations skills, I found myself ready for a new challenge. I knew I wanted to pursue a complete 180-degree change in direction, but I also wanted to utilize the valuable expertise I gained while serving in the military. That's when I discovered the exciting world of real estate.

The process of buying and selling properties has always captivated me. The fast-paced nature of the real estate market reminded me of the high-pressure situations I faced in the military. As I learned more about the industry, I realized that it would be the perfect way for me to continue helping people in a different way. By helping individuals and families achieve the American dream of homeownership, I could apply the skills I honed in the Army to make a meaningful impact on people's lives.

As a real estate agent, I am humbled by the opportunity to assist clients from all walks of life in pursuing their goals. There's something special about being a part of the process that leads to someone becoming a property owner - it's an essential part of the American Dream, and I'm honored to play a role in making it a reality.

To show my dedication to my clients, I wear a bow tie on closing days to symbolize my concierge style of real estate service. I believe that every client deserves personalized attention and a commitment to going above and beyond to help them achieve their goals.

I'm also proud to be a part of the TIES Team, a group of full-time professionals who share my vision of Trust, Integrity, Expertise, and Service. We prioritize our clients' needs and work tirelessly to ensure they meet their real estate goals. I'm grateful to work alongside such dedicated professionals and look forward to continuing to make a positive impact on people's lives through real estate.

Conversation with David Abrahams

Looking back, were there any signs or clues that you had the real estate agent gene in your DNA?

Dave Abrahams: When I look back, I realize that the experience of buying and selling homes while moving around the country with the Army was quite enjoyable for me. I loved asking questions and learning from the real estate agents I worked with during those transactions. As I thought about my next career move after my Army service, becoming a real estate agent was one option I had already considered. I discovered that many skills required for success in real estate are also cultivated during a military career, which made the profession even more fascinating.

Being a real estate agent requires various skills that I found to be present in my military career. I learned to be detail-oriented and to pay attention to important information while working in the Army. Similarly, it is crucial to read and understand contracts and other legal documents in real estate. The ability to communicate effectively with clients and colleagues is another important skill I developed during my time in the military, which has proven invaluable as a real estate agent.

Can you briefly describe the person you were before being a real estate agent?

Dave Abrahams: Before I joined the Army, some experiences helped shape who I am today. I grew up in a very small town called Forks, Washington, which some readers with teenage daughters might recognize as the setting for the Twilight Series. However, before vampires and werewolves, it was just my family and me living on a little farm outside of town. I always tended to talk too much or not reach my full potential, as noted in every report card from kindergarten until high school graduation. I wasn't sure what to do with my life, so I enlisted in the Army in 1987.

I was recruited to wrestle at several colleges but didn't feel like a junior college wrestler because of my arrogance at the time. So, I enlisted in the Army and was lucky enough to be recruited for active duty from there. I spent a few years in the enlisted ranks at West Point before eventually wrestling and spending four years there. It was a complete turnaround from my high school days, and many of my former teachers were surprised that I had accomplished it. I have to credit my parents for having faith in me. After graduating from West Point, I spent another 26 years in the Army, rising to the rank of Colonel before retiring in 2019.

My experiences in the Army prepared me for my current career in real estate. As an infantry enlisted officer, my job was very people-centric. Many roles in the military involve managing systems and technology, but as an infantry officer, the top priority was taking care of the soldiers under my command. I led large groups of people and managed various projects, which helped prepare me for my work in real estate. My time in the

Army taught me valuable lessons in leadership and management that have proven to be crucial in my current career.

What inspired you to make that decision to become a real estate agent?

Dave Abrahams: In 2017-2018, I was deployed to Kandahar, Afghanistan, for the third time. During my time there, some people called me the mola of Kandahar, and others referred to me as the mayor of Kandahar. It was challenging for my family when I got deployed for the third time, and I decided to retire when I returned. Although I could have stayed in the Army for another five years, I knew I didn't want to leave my family behind again.

After retiring at the end of 2019, I had almost two years to think about what I would do next. I discovered that many Facebook and LinkedIn groups of consultants are dedicated to helping people transition from the military, and I read a lot of literature about what people do when they leave. Initially, I wasn't thinking about becoming a real estate agent, but I wanted to serve, continue to serve, and get away from the government. I realized that people have a lot of turmoil after leaving the military because they get a job and hate it, quit, and then start another job that they also end up hating. I studied this phenomenon and learned it's mainly about the lifestyle you want, your purpose, and how people view you.

After thinking about what guided me, I wanted autonomy, the ability to serve, and the opportunity to be rewarded for my work. I almost bought a franchise but decided against it because although you're an independent business owner, you're still beholden to the franchise. Instead, I looked at the city government, but I didn't want to jump into the middle of some hierarchy that put a false ceiling on me. All of these things led me to real estate, where I could have autonomy, grow a team the way I want, and learn from the best in the business at Phyllis Rounding Company and around the world.

After 32 years of basic structure and hierarchy in the military, it feels good to have more freedom and control over what I do and how I do it. I am growing a beard because I couldn't grow one for 32 years, but I still get up every day and work out. I'm getting better at blocking my calendar. The things that made me successful in the military are still with me and will make me successful wherever I go.

How did your family and friends react when you decided that you were going all in on real estate?

Dave Abrahams: I find it funny to think back to when my wife Carolyn, who is a very wise woman, warned me that real estate agents usually work on nights and weekends. At the time, I thought I could eventually avoid those hours, but I still find myself working during those times. However, I do make sure to take time off when I need it. I often let people know that I won't be working for the next few days. Even though it's been a busy time, it's much better than being in Afghanistan. At least Carolyn and I get to sleep in the same bed at night.

My family was thrilled when I started my real estate career. Unfortunately, my mom passed away this year, but she and my dad always believed in me, even when I was a terrible student in high school and did some crazy things. They saw potential in me that I didn't see in myself.

My friends have also been very supportive and excited for me. They have been the foundation of my business, and I'm grateful for their help. Some of my classmates from West Point are also real estate agents across the country. We have a tight-knit community that supports and mentors each other. Some of these agents are much younger than me but are incredibly talented and use technology to their advantage. I've learned a lot from them and other experienced agents.

Starting a new career requires humility. Even if you were successful in a previous career, you have to start from the bottom again. Humility is the key to success. When people stop being humble, they often fall from the top. They believe they know everything, and that's when they stop learning. It's important to be open to learning from others, regardless of their age or experience level.

Have you had any failures that contributed to the success that you're seeing today?

Dave Abrahams: When I look back, there are many things I wish I had done differently. Sometimes it's a small mistake, like saying something in a way that causes an emotional reaction I didn't intend in a meeting. But I learn from those experiences every day.

I've also had some major failures in my life, like my failed marriage. Through that experience, I learned a lot about relationships, being a better person, and managing my money. Unfortunately, I also accumulated a tremendous amount of debt, and in my mid-thirties, I had to start over. It was a big challenge for me. When I was moving up the ranks in the military, I realized I could have managed my relationships better. I was passed over for promotion to full colonel, which was a setback. However, retiring as a lieutenant colonel was still a successful career, and I learned that no matter what level you're at, there is always something to learn from others.

In real estate, I had my first listing from the owners of Lave, one of my teammates. They had flipped a house in San Antonio, and it was my first licensed listing. However, despite the market being on fire in late 2019, we couldn't sell it. We had 150 showings but no contracts. We kept trying to fix little things based on feedback from potential buyers, but it wasn't enough. Eventually, we staged the house and retook the photos, and it sold immediately. This experience taught me the importance of presenting a property in the best possible way, regardless of its value or condition. For example, I recently listed a property that needs foundation work and has holes in the walls. But we still ensured it was clean and staged with furniture, so it looked its best.

Can you describe your current business and the types of people that you help? For example, what's it like being Dave Abrahams, a real estate agent, today?

Dave Abrahams: In 2019, I had a couple of real estate transactions, but in 2020, things really took off. Throughout that year, I completed over 30 transactions worth a little over 10 million dollars and was named the Phyllis Browning Company Rookie of the Year for 2020. I was one of the few rookies who had done $10 million worth of business in the company's 30-year history. In 2021, I wanted to double my business, so I brought on Rich Bailey to my team. Together we completed 57 transactions worth $21.7 million. Our goal for 2022 was $30 million.

I work with Rich, a retired warrant officer, and Danielle, an active-duty spouse with three kids who does all our backend stuff, including transaction coordinating. She can work from anywhere, making her an excellent addition to our team. Working together in 2021, we learned that once you have more than 50 or 60 transactions in a year, you need to put different people in charge of groups of transactions to ensure all clients receive the care they need. That's when we created the Abrams Real Estate Ties team.

We added Valerie Adams, a former Army spouse with real estate experience around the country, and Tim Culpepper, a retired Army Lieutenant Colonel who helps with digital marketing. We also brought on Lebec, a former army officer and tech executive with 10 years of experience. I work closely with Amanda Rivera, an excellent agent in San Antonio, who helps us understand the non-military side of things. We also work with Close Brown and Company.

I wear a bow tie whenever I close a deal. It's a symbol of respect for my clients, who are making the most significant transaction of their lives. It shows that I'm serving them and want them to feel comfortable and confident. You can see me wearing my bow tie on social media with the hashtag #IOnlyCloseinBows.

We decided that the logo for our team should have our values at its core. The most important thing in any position like this is trust. Our logo spells TIES: Trust, Integrity, Expertise, and Service. If you serve your clients with expertise and integrity, you'll earn their trust.

Today we have a team of five active agents and a full-time admin on staff. We work on three to eight transactions at any given time, depending on the season. We are always available for anyone interested in buying or selling real estate, whether they're ready now or just considering it for the future.

What are your hobbies, and who do you spend your non-business time with?

Dave Abrahams: I spend most of my time working, but when I'm not at work, I love spending time with my wife and child. When I'm not in San Antonio, I fly to Washington to spend time with my 81-year-old dad. My brother and sister also live in Washington. My brother owns and operates a logging company worth roughly $10 million. He didn't go to college but started running the company when he was 19. My sister runs a fitness company that she started 20 years ago.

Before working in real estate, I told my brother and sister I would be as successful as them someday. I believe that you can't consider yourself successful until you start and run your own company. While that's not necessarily true, there is something about being responsible for the success or failure of a company that's a big deal.

When I have free time, I like to go fishing. I fish for Salmon in the Pacific Northwest and speckle trout and redfish in the intercoastal in South Padre Island. I'll also play a little golf in town to recharge. Sometimes, I'll go to one of the card houses and donate a couple hundred dollars to the professional poker players, but I don't go enough to be good enough at it. It's one of the few things I'll do by myself for fun.

I love spending time with my family, and I support my son, Maze, a senior at Cole High School, in his extracurricular activities. It's like having another part-time job, but it's all worth it.

I'm also a board director for two different charitable organizations. The first one is the Captain Joseph House Foundation, which means a lot to me. Captain Joseph Schultz was a special forces officer killed in Afghanistan, and his mother converted her bed and breakfast into a respite home for Gold Star families. Essentially, it's an all-expense-paid trip for Gold Star families to spend a week together in the house, getting to know each other and helping each other quantify what life looks like after the loss of their soldiers, moving on with honor of the folks that die. So that's the Captain Joseph House Foundation.

The second organization is the Veteran Mentor Project, Inc. (VMPI), a startup veteran mentoring organization. It was started by the brother of a West Point classmate who committed suicide after he left the military. The idea is for folks struggling with life after the military to be able to make that transition. It's not just for veterans; it's also for first responders. We assign mentors to work with them through the transition process.

I'm also active in a local organization, Wear Blue: Run to Remember, another gold star benefit. It was started by a lady named Lisa Hallett when her husband was killed in Afghanistan on a deployment in 2009.

How can we learn more about David Abrahams in your real estate business and continue following your journey? How can they reach you?

Dave Abrahams: You can find me on social media platforms like Instagram, Facebook, and LinkedIn. Additionally, you can visit my website at www.realestateties.com. If you choose to like and follow me on social media, you may have the chance to watch me on the American Dream TV Network. Recently, I was selected to host a five-minute episode every other month in San Antonio. The show focuses on the lifestyle and culture of the city, and I will be showcasing some of my favorite spots in my first episode. I highly recommend that you check out the American Dream TV Network to catch a glimpse of my work.

About David Abrahams

Proudly wearing the uniform of a Soldier since 1987, David Abrahams rose from Private to Colonel during 32 years in the United States Army. With a Bachelor of Science from the United States Military Academy at West Point and a master's degree in leadership and planning, David's passion for service and lifelong learning and innovation allows him to serve his customers well in the rapidly changing world of real estate.

After buying and selling homes in Washington, Florida, and Texas, David developed a thorough understanding of prioritizing and articulating requirements throughout the home buying and selling process. He's refined this process in dozens of transactions supporting clients at all price points and in residential and commercial real estate. With experience in project management and effective operation oversight, David's executive background facilitates decision-making, optimizing time and money while minimizing risk.

In his downtime, you can find David spending quality time with family, volunteering as a board director for Captain Joseph House Foundation, a charity benefitting Gold Star Families, or saltwater fishing, chasing the Texas Inshore Slam.

WEBSITE
RealEstateTies.com

EMAIL
dabrahams@phyllisbrowning.com

FACEBOOK
Facebook.com/davidabrahamsrealtor

INSTAGRAM
Instagram.com/dabrahams.realtor

San Antonio's HVAC Expert

Airtegrity Comfort Solutions is a company that was born out of a passion for customer service and a desire to go beyond the traditional HVAC industry. Our CEO, Francisco Bermudez, envisioned a company that not only provides exceptional service but also impresses our customers with the level of expertise, dedication, and innovation we bring to the table.

At Airtegrity, we take pride in serving the San Antonio community and exceeding our customers' expectations. We understand that a well-maintained HVAC system is essential for the comfort and well-being of our customers. That's why we strive to provide the highest quality service, using the latest technology and techniques to ensure your system operates at peak performance.

Our team of skilled technicians has years of experience in the industry and undergoes rigorous training to stay up-to-date with the latest advancements in HVAC technology. We take a personalized approach to every job, taking the time to understand your unique needs and providing tailored solutions that fit your budget.

Airtegrity is not just focused on providing excellent service; we're also committed to helping you save money. Inefficient and broken climate systems can be costly to operate, and our team is dedicated to helping you save hundreds, even thousands of dollars in energy bills over time. We believe that maintaining your system is a smart investment that pays off in the long run.

So, whether you need routine maintenance, emergency repairs, or a complete system overhaul, Airtegrity is here to help. Our commitment to customer satisfaction and passion for innovation sets us apart from the rest. Join the many satisfied customers who have chosen Airtegrity as their go-to HVAC provider and experience the difference for yourself.

Conversation with Francisco Bermudez Jr

Were there any signs or clues that you might have had that entrepreneurial gene in your DNA, specifically, the HVAC business owner gene?

Francisco Bermudez: I learned my entrepreneurial spirit from my dad. Growing up, it was just me and my two younger brothers, and since I was the oldest, my dad would take me to work with him to help my mom with the other kids. That's how I learned how to work at a very young age and not only learn but also make some money. I loved earning money, even though my payment was just a hamburger. My dad would tell me that the hamburger was my payment for helping him out. But I was happy with it because we would use the money that we earned to buy snacks and other things we liked. Even though I only received a humble burger, it made me feel rich as a 10-year-old. When I had extra money to spend, it was a big deal to me. It made me feel like an adult.

I had the chance to watch my dad closely and learn from him. He would teach me the basics of his work, like when he and his team would work up in the attics. I was their helper, and although I didn't have any special skills, I would help by grabbing drinks from the ice chest or playing with the tools from their toolbox. Sometimes I would even grab beers for them because drinking while you worked was acceptable back then. I didn't have a choice since they would pick me up from school and take me to work. But even at a young age, I learned the value of working and making money.

My brothers and I were never given anything for free. We had to work for everything we wanted. If we wanted new pants or wanted to play on the soccer team, we knew we had to earn it. We would save up to buy the things we wanted. It wasn't easy, but it taught us the importance of hard work and saving our money.

What kind of student were you?

Francisco Bermudez: When I finished high school, I didn't have any plans to go to college, but I was lucky to get a scholarship to play soccer at Texas College and then later at Our Lady of the Lake. Although I hadn't studied much in high school, I discovered my passion for business, which became my major. I think they placed me in that major because I had no idea what I wanted to study. I thought I would start my own business in construction or air conditioning. But because they said I had to go to college, I played soccer and fell in love with business accounting, marketing, and administration.

I never received As in high school, but when I got to college, I earned As in all my business classes. It was so much fun and engaging for me.

What inspired you to decide that you were going to become a(n) HVAC Business Owner?

Francisco Bermudez: I have always been a risk-taker. Everyone wanted me to have a stable job, so we were looking for stability after I graduated and got married. I ended up working for the Bronxville PUB, which is a utility company. Although the pay was good, I was always in the office and felt my capabilities were limited. If I had a great idea to improve the department or the company, I was always told to keep it to myself. They told me to just come to work and not question why we've been doing the same process for 20 years when we have new technology. It was discouraging because I wanted to be the most efficient person and help our department be more efficient.

That company didn't value my efforts, so I quit and became a teacher for third and fifth grade in San Antonio. I went into teaching to build leaders for tomorrow, focusing on their leadership skills and empowering them to achieve their goals, whether in college or professionally. However, teaching wasn't what I expected. The pay wasn't really good, and I felt like we were following a curriculum that didn't reflect the skills or growth of the students. We were basing the students' growth on standardized tests instead of acknowledging their different sets of skills. I felt like we were just teaching them how to take a test, and I didn't like that because I saw the potential for growth and skills that weren't being measured properly in the school system. After three years, I was stressed out, felt like I was putting in many hours, and wasn't compensated for my efforts.

When I was a teacher, my friends who were also teachers would invite me to their homes to fix their air conditioning since I had experience with fixing them as a kid. I made $200-$300 every time I went out to fix an AC, which was pretty good. Before I quit teaching, I discovered that many of my colleagues had hired someone to fix their ACs and had paid a lot of money for a service that wasn't done correctly. I saw an opportunity to start an honest and good HVAC company in San Antonio that could provide high-quality service to customers. That's the basis of entrepreneurship: solving problems. Although many HVAC companies already existed, I saw a problem within the niche. I felt like I could fill a void by providing high-quality customer service and building a business. It was kind of sad that the HVAC industry was that bad, but it also created opportunities for me.

Tell me about the reactions from your wife, parents, and maybe even friends once you announced that you were going full-time with HVAC.

Francisco Bermudez: It was tough when I decided to leave my teaching job. My wife and I had just welcomed a newborn daughter, and I didn't want to endure the stress that came with being a teacher for another year. But I knew that I had a family to support. So, when I left, I told myself that we would succeed and make it work no matter what. However, it wasn't as smooth as I thought it would be.

Tell us about your first experience as a(n) HVAC Business Owner and how it turned out.

Francisco Bermudez: I remember one Christmas holiday when my wife and I were buying groceries, and we hadn't been paid for a job yet. All the money that we had saved was put towards that job. I tried to pay for our groceries with my debit card, but it was declined. I ran out of money and didn't want to ask my parents for help. That's when a lady shopping behind us offered to pay for our groceries. She paid for about a hundred dollars' worth of groceries, and I felt embarrassed because I had put my family through so much.

My wife and I are college graduates, and I felt I had failed them. On my side of the family, we value hard work and perseverance; on the other, they value stability and retirement. Despite the difference in values, I received a lot of support from everyone. It wasn't always easy, but we kept pushing through.

Have you experienced any failures that you now realize directly contributed to the success you have today?

Francisco Bermudez: When I started my company, I made the mistake of bringing on a few people who weren't a good fit. This affected me because I was always trying to help people. Additionally, I didn't have good control over our finances, and we weren't keeping track of where our money was going. Unfortunately, during the first year, one of the people we had hired lost $40,000 that he had taken with him. He acquired the money through our business and resold it to another vendor.

I learned that it's crucial to keep control and not trust everybody. One of the technicians I hired wasn't the right fit for us, but I wanted to give him a chance and support him as much as possible. It took me three years to realize that he wasn't the right fit, and it was hard to separate from him. But those were valuable lessons that I needed to learn.

In the beginning, we were always fair and honest with our customers. It's essential to me that if we say we're going to do something, we do it and do it right. Quality work and ensuring the customer is satisfied is a big part of our brand. When we go to customers' homes, we want to ensure they get what they paid for.

During the first year, I didn't always quote jobs properly and would lose money. But I didn't change my price or go back on my word. I learned from my mistakes and grew from them.

What is it like being the Francisco Bermuda Jr that you are today?

Francisco Bermudez: I have some strengths that I'm proud of. I'm really good at building relationships with people, working well in a team, and setting high expectations for myself and others. It's something that comes naturally to me, and I enjoy doing it. However, I must admit that I'm not very good at managing things. I struggle with following through on goals that I've set, and sometimes things can fall by the wayside. Thankfully, I have a great manager who is able to help me with this. He complements my skills by giving the team a vision and motivating them. I've found that having someone to balance me out has been really helpful.

I also want to share that I have ADHD and ADD. This means that I can be forgetful at times, and if I say I'm going to do something, I might not do it at that exact moment. I really enjoy playing golf and watching soccer games, but sometimes it can distract me from my work. This is where having someone to hold me accountable comes in. It has been really helpful for me to have someone who can help me stay on track and be successful.

Also, my faith is really important to me. There have been times when things have been really tough, like when we didn't know if we would have enough money to make payroll. But I've learned to trust in God that everything will work out in the end. Sometimes, we get a call at the last minute and it's just enough for us to make it through. We've never missed a meal, and I'm grateful for that. I believe that having faith is a big part of being successful in life.

What do you do to recharge from business, and who do you spend your non-business time with?

Francisco Bermudez: I used to be a professional soccer referee until last year. It was my favorite way to spend my free time. I always made sure to work out in the mornings before starting my day. Spending time with my wife and daughter is also very important to me. My daughter is seven years old now, and I know that time flies by so quickly. I want to make the most of the time we have together while she's young. That's why I always ask myself, "What can I do this week to make it worth it for her?"

My focus is mostly on my family. I love spending time with them and making memories. I started playing golf last year, so now I try to play at least once a week or twice a week. Golf is a fun new hobby for me, but nothing is more important than spending time with my loved ones.

About Francisco Bermudez Jr.

Francisco Bermudez is an entrepreneur and the founder of Airtegrity Comfort Solutions, a company specializing in providing exceptional AC services to residents and businesses in San Antonio. With his passion for customer satisfaction, Francisco has built a reputation as a reliable and trustworthy expert in the HVAC industry.

Francisco's love for the HVAC industry started at a young age when he would watch his father work on AC units. He developed an interest in the field, and after completing his education, he started working as a technician for an HVAC company. He gained valuable experience and knowledge in the field, which he used to start his own company, Airtegrity Comfort Solutions, in San Antonio.

As the founder of Airtegrity Comfort Solutions, Francisco Bermudez has always been dedicated to delivering high-quality services to his customers. He understands the importance of having a comfortable living or working environment and strives to ensure that his team provides the best AC solutions to achieve this.

With his vast experience and expertise, Francisco and his team of experts at Airtegrity Comfort Solutions offer comprehensive AC services, including installation, repair, and maintenance. They use the latest tools and techniques to ensure that every job is done efficiently, effectively, and in minimal time to minimize disruptions to their clients' daily routines.

Francisco Bermudez and his team at Airtegrity Comfort Solutions have built a loyal customer base thanks to their commitment to customer satisfaction. They are always ready to go above and beyond to ensure that their clients' AC units are in excellent condition and operate efficiently, prolonging their lifespan.

If you need expert AC services in San Antonio, remember the name Airtegrity Comfort Solutions, and rest assured that Francisco Bermudez and his team will take care of all your AC needs.

WEBSITE
AirtegrityCS.com

FACEBOOK
Facebook.com/airtegritycs

EMAIL
helpdesk@airtegritycs.com

LINKEDIN
LinkedIn.com/in/fbjr005

San Antonio's Trusted CPA

Marco Flores is the owner of MFCPA, P.C., which provides outstanding service to its clients through dedication to three underlying principles that guide their work: professionalism, responsiveness, and quality.

With over 25 years of experience serving individuals, businesses, and non-profit organizations, MFCPA takes great pride in being a valuable resource to its clients. MFCPA offers a wide range of services that extend well beyond tax return preparation.

By investing in the latest technologies, MFCPA ensures they provide their clients with the highest quality service possible. Secure file sharing, cloud data storage, and electronic tax return filing are just a few features that allow MFCPA to serve clients with unmatched efficiency.

Tax return preparation and accounting can be time-consuming and challenging, so MFCPA offers clients peace of mind by handling their tax and accounting needs. This allows our clients to focus on the things that are important to them.

Responsiveness and communication are critical, so MFCPA prioritizes promptly addressing questions and concerns. Explaining complex concepts in layman's terms allows MFCPA's clients to make informed decisions about their finances.

Conversation with Marco Flores

Looking back, were there any signs or clues that you might have the CPA gene in your DNA?

Marco Flores: When I think back to my childhood, I was really into baseball and collecting baseball cards. I found it amusing that people collect cards just for fun, but I would read the backs of the cards. I loved looking at batting averages and studying all those numbers and was genuinely interested in that.

Although I loved numbers and was always good at math, I had never heard of accounting. Accounting is not just math; it's more about working with numbers to make sense of them. There's the numerical aspect, but also the organizational element. I have always been an organized person. I prefer things to be where I can find them, and I've always been good at working with numbers.

I planned to become a physical therapist since I wanted to do something in sports. But, when I got to college, I stumbled upon accounting and realized that this has always been my talent. I could make money doing it, so why not pursue it?

What kind of jobs did you have before being a CPA?

Marco Flores: I wasn't always the best student when I was younger. I grew up in Lansing, Michigan, and attended a public school. My dad thought I was a bit of a troublemaker, so he decided to send me to a private school. It turned out that getting into trouble in private school was easier, but somehow, I managed to finish eighth grade. Then, my family and I moved to Texas. My dad always told me I was intelligent, but I didn't apply myself in school. Now that I have a 12-year-old and a 15-year-old, I tell them the same thing. I see myself in them.

The other day, I talked with my son's basketball coach, who also happened to be my high school basketball coach. He told me my son reminded him a lot of me when I was younger. My son is smart, but like me, he has difficulty staying focused, especially at his age. I wasn't a bad kid, but I did have a bit of a rebellious streak. My wife always knew that I wasn't meant to work for someone else; I was meant to be my own boss. I finished high school and college and started working, but I was never really happy.

I started working when I was 16, taking various jobs like working in fast food and a call center. I lasted only a month at the call center because I didn't want to follow the script, so they let me go. Eventually, I found my calling in accounting and taxes. I realized I could be good at it but didn't want to put money in other people's pockets. I didn't want to work 78 to 80 hours a week for someone else to profit from my hard work. I wanted to do it for myself. So, in 2014, I started my own business. It's been almost ten tax seasons now. Sometimes, life takes us in directions that we never could have imagined. If someone had asked me if I saw myself as a CPA when I was younger, I probably would have said no way. But here I am. Many people have ideas, but life can take us in different directions. It's not always the path we intended or planned, but it can still lead us to where we need to be.

What inspired you to take the bookkeeper or the CPA route?

Marco Flores: I realized that kinesiology was not the right fit for me, so I decided to switch my major to general business. You must take finance, marketing, and accounting courses as a business major. I remember taking a tax class and looking at the other students around the classroom. I noticed that many weren't engaged and were only there because they needed the credit to graduate. However, I found the subject fascinating. It seemed like a unique niche, and I was the only one in the room who seemed interested.

I realized that when we graduated and entered the working world, most of my classmates would be working in marketing, finance, or something other than taxes. Talking about taxes with others can be challenging because it's like speaking a different language. I understand why people would want nothing to do with it, but for me, it was different. As a CPA, taxes became my passion. That tax class was like a light bulb going off in my head. It was then that I realized that working with taxes was my calling.

What was the reaction you received from your family and friends once you told them you wanted to be CPA? Were they encouraging and supportive, or did they think you were crazy?

Marco Flores: Most of my friends weren't really into academics and didn't want to go to college. However, my family, especially my dad, always emphasized the importance of education. He believed education was the key to giving us the life we had growing up. So, he always encouraged me to focus on my studies. Even though some people think of accountants as boring bean counters who never go outside or do anything, I don't fit that stereotype. Sometimes, I even surprise myself. I don't wear glasses or have a calculator in my pocket protector. People are often surprised when they find out that I'm an accountant. However, I enjoy my job and the opportunities it has provided for my family and me.

While I'm interested in personal investments, accounting will always be my bread and butter.

Have you experienced any failure that has contributed to your success today?

Marco Flores: I could write a book on my failures alone; it would be like an encyclopedia. That's why I tell myself and others that if I'm not failing, I'm not trying. I need to fail, make mistakes, and screw up. Of course, I don't want to do anything monumental, like a life-changing mistake, but I have to try things out. It's all about trial and error, and that's just how life is. I mean, I have made so many mistakes, both personally and professionally, as an employee, a boss, a husband, a father, and a son. But I know that I am imperfect, and that is okay.

Every time I make a mistake, there are wins and lessons to be learned. I have made some big ones and need to learn from them. I have had to live on rice and beans because it's a part of growth and a marathon, not a sprint. I tell myself and others that it's a marathon. Everyone wants to see immediate results and get rich quickly, but it's not like that. It's a grind every single day. I have to grind if I want to get better at something, and I'll have bad days; I'll have days where I take two steps back. But I have to put that behind me, learn from it, and move on because there's always tomorrow.

Please briefly describe your current business model, the types of people you help, and the problems you solve.

Marco Flores: Currently, there's a high demand for accountants, and it's an excellent time to become one. People need our services now more than ever. Many older CPAs are retiring, and younger ones are transitioning to finance, making this an advantageous time to be an accountant.

As a small business owner, I understand the daily struggles of juggling many tasks. You have to be involved in sales and marketing while ensuring the technical work is completed. You have to handle payroll, HR, and many other responsibilities. Therefore, I enjoy working with other small business owners who experience the same challenges.

Although I have a few $20 million clients, most have businesses that earn less than one or two million dollars a year. While that might sound like a lot of money, when you consider the expenses involved in running a business, you may only be breaking even or even losing money. This is why I am most passionate about helping people identify areas where they can improve. By recognizing where they are earning more money, they can focus on those areas to help their business grow.

Being a business owner has its ups and downs, just like life. Navigating those ups and downs is an invaluable experience that I want to share with others.

What do you do when you are not working? What are your hobbies? Who do you spend your non-business time with?

Marco Flores: I don't have a big group of friends, but I have my family and a few close friends. My work keeps me busy all year round, not just during tax season, and it often means working evenings and weekends. However, I always prioritize attending my kids' basketball games and school events.

To be honest, I'm a homebody now. I don't need to go out and party like I did when I was younger. Spending time with my family is what I enjoy the most. We like to relax, watch movies, go out to dinner, and just be together. We don't take extravagant vacations because our businesses demand much of our time and attention, but we spend quality time together while our kids are still young.

We often have family nights where we eat dinner at home, watch a movie, and play video games together. It's essential to decompress and take a break from work because being a small business owner, husband, and father is demanding. Burnout can happen, so we need to make time for relaxation.

One of the best things about being self-employed is the freedom to take time off when needed. For example, if I want to take my boys to the movies, I can just do it. I don't have to worry about getting permission from a boss or pretending to be sick. It's priceless to spend that time with my family whenever we want.

If you could go back in time and give the pre-successful version of yourself one piece of advice, what would that be?

Marco Flores: I should've started my business sooner. I believe God has a plan for all of us, and I should have followed that plan earlier. It's important to appreciate the people with you and not take them for granted. I stay focused and do not get sidetracked by things that won't help me or my family. Looking back, I realize that some things I did were not smart, but I didn't know any better then. Making mistakes is part of life and how we learn and grow.

Mistakes can be painful and not enjoyable, but they shape us into who we are today. When we learn from our experiences, we gain wisdom, and that can be a beautiful thing. However, to gain wisdom, we often must endure difficult times. But as long as we are alive, we can keep moving forward and doing what we need to do. We are truly blessed, and we shouldn't complain. God is good, and God is great.

How can we learn more about you and your CPA practice and continue following your journey?

Marco Flores: You can find me on Google if you search for my name. I work at a firm with an office, but we're becoming more of a virtual firm. However, we have an internet presence, so you can always find us online. I'm always available for phone calls or Zoom meetings if you need to talk to me. Some people prefer to meet in person, and I'm open to that too.

If you want to learn more about our firm, visit our website at www.mfcpatx.com. The website provides more information about who we are and what we do. It's not just a marketing tool. I believe the best way to get to know somebody is to do business with them. So if you're looking for a CPA or thinking about switching CPAs, you can give me a call. We can chat, get to know each other better, and see if we're a good fit. And if we're not, that's perfectly fine too.

About Marco Flores

MFCPA San Antonio, P.C. is a well-known accounting firm serving businesses in San Antonio for almost a decade. The firm provides top-notch CPA and general accounting services to businesses, individuals, and non-profits across various industries. Marco Flores, the owner of MFCPA, works closely with his clients to provide personalized services that help them improve their financial management and save money during tax season.

With a keen understanding of industry regulations, MFCPA takes the time to get to know each of its clients, enabling the team to tailor their services to meet their unique needs. Marco Flores and his team are committed to providing cost-effective services and use simple terminology to ensure that their clients understand the work being done for them. They are also quick to respond to any inquiries or concerns, ensuring their clients feel supported and informed throughout the process.

MFCPA uses the latest technological advances, including QuickBooks and cloud-based apps, to provide secure and organized accounting processes. This is particularly beneficial for busy business owners who need reliable, streamlined systems to manage their finances effectively.

In addition to accounting services, MFCPA offers financial planning and tax preparation services to help businesses plan for the future and manage their taxes efficiently. Marco Flores is dedicated to the well-being of his customers and works tirelessly to help them save money while providing excellent service.

Overall, MFCPA San Antonio, P.C. is a trusted and reliable accounting firm offering comprehensive services to businesses, individuals, and non-profits. With a focus on personalized service, cost-effectiveness, and the latest technological advancements, MFCPA is well-equipped to help its clients achieve financial success.

WEBSITE
mfcpatx.com

EMAIL
marco.flores@mfcpatx.com

FACEBOOK
Facebook.com/mfcpasanantonio

A Concise Introduction to Tax-Saving Trusts

Sally Gimon shares her expertise and insights and sheds light on the concepts surrounding tax-saving trusts. She explains the difference between family trusts and the specialized spendthrift trust she works with, which has historical origins and operates within the framework of federal contract law.

Sally highlights how these trusts offer substantial opportunities for federal tax savings, cater to various professions and investments, and provide privacy protection and safeguarding against judgments. Furthermore, she addresses common misconceptions, clarifies how funds can be accessed, and offers advice for individuals evaluating trusts.

Conversation with Sally Gimon

Could you please explain your role and how you assist your clients?

Sally Gimon: I specialize in helping clients minimize federal taxes through a unique spendthrift trust. In the United States, about 97% of trusts are family trusts. These trusts are primarily designed to avoid probate after someone passes away but don't continue across generations and cannot be utilized again. The type of trust I work with originated in England during the time of King Henry the Eighth. It emerged when King Henry faced challenges for beheading his wife and subsequently sought to establish authority over the Lords and ladies by establishing the Church of England. This trust draws upon historical precedents, including the Magna Carta, and operates within the framework of federal contract law.

The business trust I specialize in offers individuals who earn a 1099 income a significant opportunity to save at least 70% on their federal taxes year after year. This applies to various professions like salespeople and affiliate marketers. On the other hand, the beneficial trust caters to investors engaged in activities such as passive investment, real estate, cryptocurrencies (investing and mining), stock market day trading, options, forex, and more. Through the beneficial trust, investors can save on capital gains (both short-term and long-term), interest income, dividend income, rental income, and royalties. Both the business trust and the beneficial trust provide substantial opportunities for federal tax savings. Moreover, these trusts offer privacy protection for your information and, most importantly, safeguard against the payment of judgments in the event of a lawsuit. While I cannot prevent you from being sued, the trust ensures you won't be liable for any judgments.

What problem does the trust solve?

Sally Gimon: The trust primarily solves the problem of organizing and structuring assets. By placing all assets within the trust, individuals can effectively avoid inheritance tax since the trust holds ownership of the assets. This creates a secure and structured environment. The trust is irrevocable, similar to the trust used by the Rockefellers, known as the Office. Their trust has a rich history spanning seven generations and includes nearly 400 beneficiaries.

One common issue I frequently come across in the realm of real estate involves the 1031 exchange. It's crucial to ensure that the 1031 exchange remains ongoing, as the tax bill becomes due once it ceases. I often encounter situations where adult children deal with incapacitated or deceased parents and suddenly face an unexpected tax bill. Many investors are also unaware that they are subject to paying short-term capital gains tax on their profits, ranging from 10-35%, depending on their tax bracket. For those selling a business, long-term capital gains tax at 15% or 20% can result in substantial amounts owed, potentially reaching thousands of dollars for some individuals.

How can the funds be accessed?

Sally Gimon: You must obtain a new Employer Identification Number (EIN) for the trust to access the funds. In the case of the business trust, this EIN will cover various expenses like your home, electricity, water, and mortgage payments. While there may be a due-on-clause for mortgages, as long as the mortgage is paid, it doesn't pose a problem. However, it's important to note that the beneficial trust does not cover general funds or food expenses.

Nevertheless, you can utilize a tax-free demand letter within the trust. This letter can be written for any amount within the trust and can be used to cover specific expenses. For example, I own a 2015 car initially purchased for $27,500. I can write a demand letter for up to $27,500 to cover my food expenses. Additionally, if you have children under 18, the trust fully covers their expenses. Furthermore, if your children are over 18 and attending college or a technical school, the trust will also pay for their education. Essentially, the trust assumes responsibility for all covered expenses.

My car is owned by the trust, and it covers various costs, such as registration fees, windshield repairs, insurance, and fuel expenses. While the trust doesn't directly save me on taxes in this instance, as a real estate investor, the funds flow through the trust, providing me with convenient access to the money.

Are there any misconceptions about how the trust operates?

Sally Gimon: There are numerous misconceptions surrounding the trust. Some people mistakenly believe it's illegal or dismiss it as a scam. I recently had a conversation with a gentleman who owns five apartment buildings in the Bronx, and even his CPA was convinced that it was illegal. In such cases, I often recommend reading the book "Scott and Ascher on Trusts, Fifth Edition," which includes an entire chapter dedicated to the spendthrift trust. This type of trust originated in England during the time of King Henry the Eighth, and the law firm I work with holds the patent for this trust. They have a trust that has been in existence for 350 years and is still going strong, passing from one generation to another. The trust operates under the principles of contract law, and it can only be changed if Congress decides to do so.

Let me provide further clarification. Let's say, hypothetically speaking, that Congress decides to change the trust on March 17th, 2024. Any Spendthrift Trusts started before that date will continue; it is a contract and cannot be changed. No new Spendthrift Trusts could be written after that date. It's important to note that this trust has been brought before the Supreme Court on two separate occasions, and in both instances, it received favorable rulings. The Supreme Court recognizes that the trust can enter into contracts and conduct business on its behalf. Therefore, the trust is as legal as it can be.

Many people fail to realize that the IRS tax code was established only in 1913, during our approach to World War I. However, this trust predates the IRS tax code, and affluent families like the Rockefellers and others ensured their long-term financial security by utilizing such trusts.

At what level of wealth would you suggest people start considering this as an option?

Sally Gimon: To explore this option, it's important to note that both the business trust and the beneficial trust require an upfront cost of $20,500. Therefore, I recommend that individuals start considering it when they have around $50,000, although it often makes more financial sense at the $70,000 mark.

I frequently collaborate with business brokers who assist in the sale of businesses. For example, I recently helped a gentleman sell a restaurant valued at $3,000,000, including all equipment, food, and recipes. By utilizing the trust structure, he saved $460,000 at a 15% tax rate or $600,000 at a 20% tax rate. The exact figures may vary, but the key point is that he saved a six-figure amount in taxes. These savings are significant, particularly for a 69-year-old individual and his 68-year-old wife, as they contribute to their retirement funds.

How did you become familiar with the trust?

Sally Gimon: I first learned about the trust through Garrett Gunderson's book titled "What Billionaires Do" (formerly titled "What Would the Rockefellers Do?"). Although the book focuses on the Rockefellers Spendthrift Trust, called the "Office," I delved into it, conducting extensive research by reaching out to people and conducting online searches. During this process, I came across a law firm in Houston that held the patent for the trust. I became their client and subsequently started teaching a mastermind within my real estate group. Real estate investors often face significant tax burdens, making this trust an attractive solution.

This discovery brought about a significant change in my life, and in March of 2022, I founded "the trust is you.com" to help as many people as possible save money. Since then, I have been assisting various investors. For example, I recently worked with a crypto investor who planned to sell some of his cryptocurrency stocks to fund his son's college education. However, he wasn't aware of the substantial capital gains tax he would incur. When he reached out to me, we set up the trust and transferred assets to his exchange, allowing him to navigate the situation more effectively.

What advice do you have for individuals evaluating trusts?

Sally Gimon: When evaluating trusts, it's crucial to understand that the majority of trusts in the United States, around 97%, serve the purpose of avoiding probate and then dissolve. In contrast, the spendthrift trust is a legally recognized trust, patented in the IRS tax code 643(b), and has been presented before the Supreme Court twice. It's essential to seek accurate and reliable information.

For example, I recently spoke with a gentleman who operates a transportation company. He believed that having an

LLC provided sufficient protection, but unfortunately, an LLC doesn't shield personal liability. In his case, he is considering establishing a business trust to minimize his personal liability. By doing so, the trust would cover insurance costs in case of an accident and any resulting damages, ensuring that he cannot be personally sued. In a country where lawsuits are prevalent, with statistics suggesting that one in three people will face a lawsuit in their lifetime, it's vital to make informed decisions and obtain the right information.

It's important to differentiate between trustworthy providers and those who may not offer comprehensive services. In my case, I work with a team that includes trust attorneys from a patent law office. I recently had a conversation with an individual who had paid a significant amount of money to a trust provider but was now unable to reach the attorney. While I'm doing my best to assist him, I don't have detailed knowledge about the specifics of his trust. However, I'm providing him with as much information as possible to guide him through the situation.

How can people access further information?

Sally Gimon: To access more information, you can visit my website, thetrustisyou.com. You'll find valuable resources and details about the trust on the website. I also host a podcast called "Stop Paying Capital Gains Now!" where I discuss relevant topics and share insights. Additionally, I conduct a live Q&A session every Monday at 8:00 PM Eastern Time. During these sessions, I go through my slide deck and address any questions participants may have. These avenues provide opportunities to learn more and gain a deeper understanding of the trust and its benefits.

About Sally Gimon

Sally was motivated to become a real estate investor when her mom became sick in October 2018. Sally was 53 and needed to make a change in her life quickly. She has been an insurance agent for 20 years and has used her experience to make positive changes. She shares information weekly in her real estate group and Win, Win Women TV.

In July 2020, she bought a bank-owned property for $20,000 that would go to auction for $50,000 when Covid restrictions were lifted. She knew her Capital Gains would be $7,140 and researched how the rich paid so little in taxes. This led her to find the Business and Beneficial Spendthrift Trusts.

WEBSITE
https://TheTrustIsYou.com

Inside the Mind of a Seasoned Business Strategist: Unveiling Key Business Insights

Regina Gulbinas is a seasoned life and business strategist with over two decades of experience. While providing valuable insights into her work and her impact on businesses, she emphasizes the importance of tapping into one's abilities and mindset to build a successful business, bridging the knowledge gap, and seeking external perspectives.

Regina addresses misconceptions about her role and highlights the obstacles that entrepreneurs face when seeking help. She showcases the transformative outcomes resulting from her guidance and expertise through a client example. Regina's dedication to empowering individuals and her emphasis on the crucial elements of people and money in business make her a trusted and sought-after strategist.

Conversation with Regina Gulbinas

Who do you help, and how do you assist them?

Regina Gulbinas: I've been a life and business strategist for 21 years. My focus as a business strategist is helping individuals tap into their full potential, develop an unstoppable mindset, and become extraordinary leaders of their organizations to build successful businesses.

During the initial 17 years of my career, I collaborated closely with CEOs, offering comprehensive guidance on managing and scaling their businesses effectively. As a seasoned strategist, my role involved meticulously evaluating the intricate details of their organizations, identifying areas in need of restructuring, and providing actionable solutions. By analyzing their operations, we gained insights into any missteps and strategized ways to rectify them, ultimately leading to restored profitability.

Supporting individuals in overcoming complex business challenges is incredibly rewarding. It allows me to assist them in preserving their employees, maintaining business momentum, and creating long-term sustainability and profitability. In the past four years, I have shifted more toward the online space while still working with offline businesses. I have developed a strong affinity for accessing the global market and leveraging my knowledge of what works and what doesn't work. I package this expertise to help businesses of all types become more profitable. I also serve online entrepreneurs, CEOs, coaches, and mentors worldwide.

What are the key benefits and advantages of your services?

Regina Gulbinas: The biggest benefit of working with me is the combination of an outside perspective and my extensive knowledge, wisdom, experience, and expertise. Business owners get access to over two decades of experience in minutes—talk about saving time to gain needed information and knowledge. As a business owner and CEO, you may have competent individuals around you, but having someone with 21 years of experience offering different perspectives, examples, and insights can be invaluable. We all have blind spots, and I can identify those blind spots and provide suggestions and strategies to save time and improve profitability significantly.

One advantage of working with a qualified and knowledgeable professional like me, particularly in business infrastructure and scaling, is gaining an external perspective. Also, emotional decisions can be very costly. By bringing in an unbiased expert with a global view of your company, and your best interest at heart, you then get rational assessments and clarity of direction. While I genuinely care about your success, I can remove the emotional aspect and take a comprehensive look at your company, identifying what works and what doesn't and showing you why.

Why do business operations suffer from an emotional attachment?

Regina Gulbinas: I have a lot of respect for anyone who takes on the journey of building a business. This takes courage! Often these brave men and women have put everything on the line. I have seen people use all their life savings, deplete home equity, and go deep into debt to chase their dream of being a business owner and hopefully becoming financially free.

CEOs, business owners, and entrepreneurs have deep emotional attachments to their companies, understandably so. This often will hinder long-term profitability when mixed with strategy. Having someone with an outside perspective, emotional detachment, ability to identify blind spots, understand revenue-generating activities, strategy, navigate relationships, and comprehend the building blocks of successful businesses will be a game-changer for your business.

What challenges do your prospects typically face when seeking your help?

Regina Gulbinas: The knowledge gap is always reflected in their numbers. Unfortunately, most people won't acknowledge their knowledge gap until it appears on their financial statements. I always emphasize that we constantly invest time or money in life and business. Instead of investing your non-replenishable resource of time, why not invest money to tap into someone else's expertise?

What are some of the main obstacles preventing people from seeking your help?

Regina Gulbinas: One of the significant obstacles I often encounter is the interference of ego.

Many individuals, driven by ego, find it challenging to ask for direction or assistance. This pattern is quite common. Often, people wait until they are in significant financial trouble before realizing they need help.

Also, in my experience, those who see it as an expense will likely wait until the last minute to ask for help. Those who see mentorship as an investment and a way to get to their desired outcome quicker will invest more actively.

We tend to believe that we know certain things unless tangible evidence forces us to question our understanding. The main obstacle is the mindset of self-reliance, where individuals think they can handle everything on their own. When we rely only on our knowledge, our company and its numbers quickly resemble our knowledge gaps.

There's a popular saying, "I don't need any assistance. I can do it on my own." However, when the lack of knowledge starts to impact a business's financial performance, with red numbers appearing on the financial statements, individuals realize something is amiss. They may think, "I'm doing everything right, the operations are running smoothly, but I'm still incurring losses." This is where outside expertise, unburdened by emotional attachment but armed with knowledge, experience, and years of investment, becomes incredibly valuable. It's essential to reach out to someone and say, "There's something wrong here. I need guidance." It's worth noting that businesses fail every day, and some even close before they have a chance to take off.

Another significant obstacle is people's reluctance to ask for help in a timely manner. Recognize one's limitations, acknowledge what they don't know, and understand the importance of seeking support. However, many individuals prioritize saving money over obtaining the necessary help. I always emphasize that not knowing what to do leads to no positive outcome. That's why mentorship and guidance are available—to provide the necessary support. Many people are hesitant to invest the required money. Still, I remind them that they are always investing something, whether it's money (a replenishable resource) or time (a non-replenishable resource). Interestingly, individuals often pay with what they value least, and this pattern is quite common. They undervalue their time and hold onto their money.

What strategies do you use to help clients overcome mindset barriers and unlock their full potential?

Regina Gulbinas: One of my key strategies is addressing the interplay between emotional and logical decision-making processes that often influence business owners, especially when facing cash flow challenges. I emphasize the importance of making long-term, logical, and profitable decisions instead of succumbing to short-term emotional impulses. To effectively convey this message, I provide clients with examples demonstrating how their previous decision-making approaches may have fallen short of their desired outcomes. They need to recognize that their current mindset may not align with their goals. Tangible proof of how their current approach limits their success often captures their attention and opens the door for me to assist in transforming their mindset.

Our decisions ultimately reflect our mindset and belief system. By analyzing the numbers, we can uncover what we truly believe is possible for ourselves. Therefore, I consider clients' historical decision-making patterns, which are influenced by their mindsets and beliefs. Working together, I guide clients toward making different, high-quality decisions from an alternative perspective and mindset. While some individuals readily embrace and implement these changes, others may require tangible evidence. Starting with small decisions, we gradually build a solid foundation for a transformed mindset.

Let's consider a construction company as an example. Many construction companies believe that a specific profit margin is the industry standard. When I propose aiming for a higher margin, such as 30-33%, they often perceive it as audacious. However, I challenge them to bid on one project at that higher margin, following my suggested approach. The goal is to create tangible evidence of the benefits of this mindset shift. Even though their current mindset may initially struggle to comprehend the possibility, their perception gradually changes as we demonstrate tangible results and provide more evidence along the way. They start bidding higher, achieving greater margins, and experiencing improved profitability. This process helps them understand that a single decision in one area can have a positive ripple effect throughout their business and life.

My strategies involve addressing the emotional versus logical decision-making process, presenting tangible evidence of how the current mindset may limit success, and gradually guiding clients toward making higher-quality decisions from a transformed perspective. By challenging existing beliefs and instilling confidence in the potential for change, clients can overcome mindset barriers and unlock their full potential.

What are the most common misconceptions business owners have that can lead to problems?

Regina Gulbinas: One of the biggest misconceptions is the belief that they can fix or scale their business entirely on their own. People often think that if they keep trying, eventually, it will work. However, if a particular approach hasn't yielded results in the past decade, it's unlikely to suddenly become successful in the next year. There's a misconception that they can recycle an idea and expect it to magically work later.

Another misconception is that they have to say yes to every job or client that comes their way, even if it doesn't align with their long-term goals or profitability. Understand that not every client is the right fit, and sometimes it's necessary to let go of current clients who are causing difficulties or not generating enough profit. Similarly, not every employee is the right fit for a company, and that's an important aspect to consider. The same applies to vendors.

These are just a few of the misconceptions I often encounter. However, one of the primary misconceptions among CEOs and business owners is the belief that they can achieve a successful 7-figure business with little information. The reality is that continuous growth requires increasing knowledge, wisdom, and education. Each level of growth necessitates filling a widening knowledge gap.

Another misconception relates to hiring decisions. CEOs sometimes focus solely on the cost of hiring without considering the necessary knowledge and skill level. They may try to save money by hiring a bookkeeper when they actually need a qualified accounting manager who can provide deeper financial analysis and help them make informed decisions based on the numbers. It's important to consider the expertise required rather than solely focusing on cost savings.

However, the biggest mistake I see CEOs make is believing they can succeed long-term without additional qualified guidance, support, and mentorship. Acquiring a bit of knowledge is not enough to sustain a business indefinitely. Each level of growth will require additional knowledge.

How do you address the knowledge gap?

Regina Gulbinas: To bridge the knowledge gap, I gently point out to individuals that their current approach hasn't yielded the desired results. Communicating this truth with kindness and respect is important, ensuring they maintain their dignity throughout the process. We discuss why their current efforts yielded current results. However, if they aspire to achieve more significant goals, it becomes evident that adjustments to their existing strategies may be necessary.

I rely on historical evidence, numbers, and tangible examples during these discussions to support my points. I don't simply state, "This isn't working." Instead, I highlight specific areas that have not produced the desired outcomes. Many individuals have not yet admitted that their current methods are ineffective because they hold onto the belief that things will eventually work out. This is why people often find themselves stuck in repetitive cycles and facing the same challenges.

The next step is to identify specific aspects that can be tweaked or improved, even if they are minor adjustments along the way. It doesn't always require a massive overhaul. By highlighting these smaller shifts that can be made in their business, production processes, or financial strategies, they can start to see immediate improvements. Even an immediate small win will help them recognize that there is a gap in their knowledge and that there are ways to enhance their operations, growth, and profitability. Moreover, when I can help them achieve a quick win up-front, they will likely gain a deeper understanding that I am the person who can guide them toward further success and beyond.

How do you help clients identify and prioritize their business goals, and what methods do you use to ensure achieving those goals?

Regina Gulbinas: To begin, I assess the current state of the company and its needs. It's essential to address any existing infrastructure issues before scaling the business. For example, if the company has low profit margins or employees are in the wrong positions, these issues must be resolved first. Building a solid foundation is crucial for long-term success, which is always my focus. Therefore, the initial step is determining whether we are scaling profitability or chaos. Most businesses have areas that require improvement or cleaning up, Enhancing Margins and Overheads

Reviewing all clients' terms and pricing optimizing employee performance maximizing productivity and profitability through skill and personality-based role allocation streamlining production efficiency and administrative workflow negotiating favorable supplier terms eradicating financial drains and bottlenecks, and so on....

Once the initial cleanup process is complete, we move on to identifying the company's desired goals. Clearly define these goals and unpack what the company aims to achieve by the end of the year. Based on the company's specific needs and growth objectives, we develop and implement procedures and strategies. We consider where the company wants to be in the next 12 months. However, note that when entering a company, there are often distractions, and the CEO may be pulled in different directions. Therefore, the CEO must become the organization's leader, ensuring alignment and fulfillment of responsibilities by everyone involved.

The process involves assessing the current state of the company, establishing clear goals, and then reverse-engineering the steps required to achieve those goals. However, for success, the CEO must align their mindset, emotional intelligence, and decision-making abilities with the agreed-upon direction. If the CEO fails to embrace necessary changes and continues to operate based on previous decision-making patterns, any implemented efforts become irrelevant.

Throughout the process, the CEO must provide leadership and ensure alignment within the organization to maximize the likelihood of achieving the established goals.

Can you explain the significance of effective communication and relationship building?

Regina Gulbinas: Certainly! Effective communication and relationship building is vital for running a successful business. I've often witnessed the negative consequences that arise when crucial discussions and topics are avoided in the pursuit of securing clients or contracts quickly. I've rarely come across a company that hasn't experienced relationship breakdowns or negative outcomes due to a lack of communication. By highlighting these instances, I can demonstrate the tangible consequences of not discussing terms upfront or failing to clarify expectations.

For instance, in the case of payment terms, I advise my clients to be transparent and clear with their clients. In the construction industry, I encourage them to establish upfront payment terms and communicate that resources will be redirected to other projects if payments are not received on time. Surprisingly, when expectations are communicated clearly, most clients align with the agreed-upon terms and pay accordingly. The key is to create a win-win environment by openly discussing expectations with clients, suppliers, employees, and management.

Clarity and understanding of expectations are essential for everyone involved in the business. Often, people hesitate to communicate their expectations due to the fear of non-compliance. However, avoiding these conversations only leads to problems and misunderstandings. Establish clarity and honesty from the beginning. What are your expectations from clients, suppliers, and everyone who interacts with your business?

Postponing uncomfortable discussions harms relationships due to a lack of clarity. It's a choice between having difficult conversations upfront or risking the relationship's collapse later. Since many businesses I work with already have a history of poor communication, strained relationships, and ineffective supplier communication, providing examples is not challenging. They have experienced the negative consequences firsthand.

When addressing mindset concerns, business owners often fear uncomfortable discussions because their clients are used to setting rules and payment timelines. Realign these relationships by establishing clear rules and boundaries for engagement. While some people may become upset or choose to leave, strict rules, boundaries, and clear expectations increase the likelihood of clients respecting and valuing your business. People are willing to pay more for the assurance and safety they feel when working with a company that demonstrates clear boundaries, expectations, and effective communication. This approach fosters respect and demonstrates true leadership.

Avoiding important discussions and failing to establish clear expectations can lead to relationship breakdowns and negative outcomes. By openly communicating expectations, setting boundaries, and practicing effective communication, businesses can foster stronger relationships, gain respect, and achieve greater success.

How do you apply these lessons in your client interactions and strategies?

Regina Gulbinas: The most important lesson I have learned is the significance of having difficult conversations while maintaining people's dignity. It's not just about the specific strategies or techniques but how I approach these discussions. Through my experience and numerous conversations, I have realized the importance of ensuring people feel respected and heard during these interactions. Merely pointing out their mistakes or past failures will not help them. They will shut down and disengage. So, before introducing new strategies or teaching sustainability, I focus on establishing a connection and gaining their willingness to listen.

In my client interactions, I emphasize effective communication as a facilitator in a way that resonates with each individual. Building trust and rapport are crucial aspects. I prioritize building genuine relationships because, at its core, business is about people. Trust is the foundation upon which tangible results are built.

When individuals realize that I treat them with respect, even when discussing their poor decisions (because we all make mistakes), they begin to trust me as their guide. Approaching these discussions with grace and kindness goes a long way. Once they trust me, they are more open to implementing my suggested strategies and navigating their business accordingly. They have fewer doubts and questions because they trust my guidance. This trust accelerates their progress toward their desired outcomes.

While you may have been seeking a more concrete example, I must emphasize that this approach goes beyond specific strategies—it is about fostering genuine relationships, understanding people, and treating them with respect. By doing so, clients open themselves to receiving guidance without constant doubt or questioning, creating an environment where they feel respected, heard, and confident that I genuinely care about their success. Also, clients are more receptive to implementing strategies and achieving their desired outcomes. Trust is at the core of our interactions, as it sets the foundation for tangible results.

Can you describe your ideal client?

Regina Gulbinas: I don't focus on a specific industry, as I have worked with diverse businesses ranging from local dance studios to commercial construction companies. I can also assist businesses globally, not limited to the United States. The common factor among all my ideal clients is their emphasis on two crucial aspects of business: people and money. Regardless of the industry, these elements form the foundation of every successful business.

For me, an ideal client takes full responsibility for their life and business. I am not interested in advocating for someone's success or engaging in arguments. It boils down to whether they genuinely want it or not. An ideal client is coachable and can engage in intelligent conversations without storming out when they hear something they may not like. This type of client aligns with my strategy-focused approach, where I prioritize bottom-line results and swift implementation.

If I find myself repeating the same information without seeing any implementation, it indicates a lack of commitment, regardless of how much they may be paying for my services. I truly love what I do and thrive on witnessing people succeed.

My ideal client is passionate about their work and cares about their employees, clients, vendors, and the quality of their products or services. They have a long-term vision and are committed to being in business for the long haul.

Can you provide an example of someone you've assisted and the outcome of your work together?

Regina Gulbinas: One memorable example is a local dance studio owner I worked with whose studio held a significant place in the community, with children growing up participating in classes and recitals. However, the owner faced challenges related to high expenses, a large rental space, and personal circumstances, including the recent passing of her husband.

Upon starting our work together, we took swift action by relocating the dance studio to a more affordable space. We initiated a comprehensive restructuring process that involved revising pricing, restructuring courses, and ensuring that the recitals could still take place. To address the financial difficulties, she opted for a Chapter 11 reorganization process, a common path for many businesses facing challenges.

Throughout the process, it was truly heartwarming to witness the incredible support from the students and parents of the dance studio. They wrote letters to the federal court judge overseeing the case, highlighting the positive impact the studio had on their lives and the community as a whole. This level of community involvement was extraordinary.

The outcome of our work together was incredibly rewarding. The dance studio owner successfully navigated the Chapter 11 process, and the studio continued to thrive. It has been approximately ten years since then, and as far as I know, she is still operating her studio. This case holds a special place in my heart due to the deep connection the local community had with the studio and its positive impact on numerous children and families.

Here is another example. One of the common challenges in this industry is maintaining profit margins. Many CEOs believe increasing margins per job is impossible and settle for lower profits as the industry norm. However, I educate my clients on breaking free from this mindset and show them alternative approaches.

In this case, the company specializes in framing, a service many other construction firms offer. Our goal was to differentiate them from the competition. We focused on key areas to stand out. First, we prioritized client experience by delivering projects on time, contrary to the belief that construction companies often miss deadlines. We also emphasized the behavior and professionalism of our employees on job sites, ensuring a clean and efficient working environment.

By providing an enhanced client experience, we built trust in our product and service, making customers willing to pay a premium. This concept applies to any industry—people value and invest more in a superior quality of experience when they trust the provider and feel confident they won't need to supervise the job constantly.

Increasing margins is just one aspect of our work. Another consideration is reducing waste within companies. Often, organizations mistakenly believe they need more staff or resources when it may not be necessary. Instead, we emphasize having a highly qualified and efficient team. More people working on a task doesn't automatically translate to increased productivity and effectiveness.

We guide CEOs in bidding on jobs differently and help them understand that not every high-paying job guarantees higher profitability. Considering the long-term perspective and evaluating where the company can truly make more money is crucial. For instance, a single $3,000,000 job may seem appealing, but it might be less profitable than multiple jobs priced at $300,000 each. We encourage CEOs to analyze the time versus money factor thoroughly. How long does it take to earn the same amount of money from a $3,000,000 job compared to several $300,000 jobs? The latter option often requires fewer staff members, less insurance coverage, reduced expenses, and less room for error during production.

To facilitate this understanding, we engage in conversations with CEOs, exploring all angles and assessing what truly generates more profit while considering the time investment. Distributing resources effectively and balancing manpower across multiple projects rather than focusing all efforts on a single job is required. We extend our teachings to the entire team, including the administration department. Time versus money is a constant consideration. We emphasize the importance of having the right personnel in each role and understanding their unique contributions.

Our approach involves teaching CEOs and their teams to comprehensively understand the inner workings of the company. This process includes analyzing profitability, optimizing resource allocation, and instilling a culture that prioritizes client experience and efficient operations collaboration.

What is the most important factor or criteria that entrepreneurs/business owners should consider before hiring a business strategist?

Regina Gulbinas: You can always tell if someone is knowledgeable in their area of expertise based on how they speak, what questions they ask you, and the solutions they offer. This alone will be a huge indicator of their values and morals. You want someone who aligns with yours. You want someone who cares about the people, not just profits. How you make your money should matter to them as much as to you.

Ask about their track record of success and expertise in their field. Thoroughly assess the strategist's experience, knowledge, and ability to deliver tangible results. Take their time to speak with them.

I recommend examining their track record. Have they worked with businesses similar to yours? Have they successfully helped other entrepreneurs overcome challenges and achieve their desired outcomes? Testimonials, case studies, and referrals from trusted sources can provide valuable insights.

Consider the strategist's expertise in areas relevant to your specific needs. Do they possess a deep understanding of your industry or niche? Can they provide tailored guidance and strategies that align with your unique business circumstances?

Another vital criterion is the strategist's approach and compatibility with your working style and values. Do they have a collaborative and supportive approach that resonates with you? Can they effectively communicate their ideas and strategies in a way you understand and feel comfortable?

Finally, trust and rapport help build a strong working relationship, which is key to a successful partnership. Trust your instincts and ensure that you feel at ease working closely with the strategist, as you will share sensitive information and rely on their expertise to drive your business forward.

How can we find out more about you?

Regina Gulbinas: To learn more about me, you can visit my website at reginagulbinas.com. I also have a presence on social media platforms like Facebook, LinkedIn, and Instagram. You're welcome to reach out, ask questions, and connect with me through these channels.

About Regina Gulbinas

Regina has worked with over 100 companies, each generating anywhere from 2-20 Million in gross annual revenue. Her objective was to teach the CEO and Management how to properly navigate every aspect of all areas within the company. Regina's function was reorganizing the CEO, taking the driver's seat, teaching the CEO how to run and grow their company correctly, and improving their cash flow. Her key focus has now gone from helping reorganize companies to helping CEOs and Entrepreneurs avoid those mistakes and decisions which bring them to financial chaos and catastrophic failure. Regina's true passion lies in helping companies grow correctly to ensure long-term success and profitability and to inspire and guide them to achieve their absolute highest potential.

WEBSITE

www.ReginaGulbinas.com/

Unveiling the Secret
of Buy/Sell Agreements

L. Paul Hood, an expert in buy/sell agreement planning, sheds light on the common deficiencies found in these agreements and the misconceptions that surround them. Hood emphasizes the importance of thorough review and drafting, as many agreements are poorly written and lack clarity. He highlights the need for business owners to understand the intricacies of their agreements, including valuation procedures, payment terms, and potential ambiguities.

Hood's extensive experience in the field and his role as a consultant and expert witness provide valuable insights into the complexities of buy/sell agreement planning.

Conversation with L. Paul Hood, Jr

Who are your clients, and how do you assist them?

Paul Hood: Many clients are business owners seeking assistance creating buy/sell agreements, as most existing agreements tend to be inadequate. Typically, it's the business owner or one of their advisors, such as a lawyer, CPA, bank trust officer, or specialized life insurance agent. There's a diverse range of professionals in this field whose clients seek to evaluate the effectiveness of their current agreements.

90% of these agreements have significant flaws and lack clarity. Many lawyers struggle to draft them effectively, as it requires expertise in entity or corporate law and tax law, which often falls into a gap area. Larger firms usually rely on either an estate planner or a corporate lawyer to handle the drafting, but they may not fully grasp the intricacies of the situation. In my capacity, I primarily work as a consultant, helping clients evaluate and enhance their buy/sell agreements. Additionally, I am proficient in writing the agreements.

How do you assist your clients in drafting improved buy/sell agreements?

Paul Hood: When I was in practice, to aid my clients in drafting better buy/sell agreements, I initiated the process by inquiring about their contingency plans for events like death or divorce. Surprisingly, many are unaware of the specifics outlined in their agreements. After signing, these agreements are often stowed away and seldom revisited. However, it is crucial to have a clear response outlined in the buy/sell agreement for each triggering event. For instance, in the event of death, there may be provisions for mandatory buy-and-sell or the option to transfer ownership to a family member. These agreements require meticulous examination from start to finish.

I encourage planners who I teach to advise their clients to read the agreement thoroughly and consider various aspects. They should ascertain if there are mandatory buy or sell provisions and determine who determines the price and the associated rules. It is also crucial to evaluate the payment terms, such as whether it will be in cash or through an installment note, and to examine provisions for interest or security, like a stock pledge or mortgage.

Regrettably, based on my extensive review of over a thousand agreements, I can confidently state that 90% have significant flaws. While most lawyers accurately address the triggering events, their mistakes often lie in the selling procedure. They may include unnecessary provisions, such as requiring the appraiser to produce a valuation within an impractical 30-day timeframe. In reality, gathering all the necessary information for an accurate appraisal within such a short period is highly unlikely. This valuation delay affects the rest of the agreement, leading to procedural defects or ambiguities that can result in legal disputes.

My role is to identify these defects and ambiguities within the agreements, guiding their clients toward crafting more comprehensive and effective buy/sell agreements.

Why are many buy/sell agreements inadequate?

Paul Hood: Many buy/sell agreements suffer from inadequacy primarily due to poor drafting and a lack of coherence. These are often crafted by individuals who lack the necessary experience and expertise to create effective agreements. In my case, I was fortunate to have worked in a 30-lawyer firm that possessed strong tax and business planning knowledge. However, being a smaller firm, we didn't have a dedicated corporate department, so the tax section also handled corporate matters. This allowed me to develop a comprehensive understanding of both tax and corporate aspects, leading me to write a book on the subject in the early 90s. I have also spoken extensively on the topic and served as an expert witness in related cases.

I frequently find myself being hired by malpractice insurance companies when an insured lawyer faces lawsuits stemming from issues within these agreements. It's a recurring pattern where poorly drafted agreements are signed, triggering events occur, and ambiguities arise between the partners. Eventually, one party files a lawsuit against the drafting lawyer for malpractice. In such cases, I often advise the insurance company to prepare for a settlement conference since taking the case to trial would likely result in a loss. The drafting lawyer involved often fails to meet the prevailing standard of practice in their jurisdiction. In some cases, they are certified tax lawyers who should be held to an even higher standard. Unfortunately, they fall short of meeting that standard, making them liable for malpractice. The insurance company must assess its exposure since they insured the lawyer's work. More often than not, I have the unfortunate task of informing them that their lawyer did not fulfill their obligations, potentially leaving them liable.

What are the misconceptions and obstacles regarding buy/sell agreement planning?

Paul Hood: One of the major misconceptions is that business owners rely solely on their lawyers for buy/sell agreement planning. They assume that since they haven't encountered any issues thus far and have an agreement in place, it must be sufficient. The main obstacle lies in persuading them to have their agreements reviewed, as they typically assume, albeit mistakenly, that their agreement is solid.

However, upon reviewing these agreements, I frequently discovered various problems and obstacles that were overlooked. For example, they may have failed to specify who will be responsible for valuing the business or overlooked the need for specialized expertise in business appraisal. There are four recognized certifications for business appraisers, and being a CPA does not automatically qualify someone unless they have specific training and experience in valuation. Sometimes, the agreements are drafted by general practitioners or individuals unfamiliar with the complexities of the matter. They may have simply copied and pasted an agreement from someone else, and the client signed it without recognizing potential deficiencies.

Business owners often assume everything is in order until a triggering event occurs. However, I emphasize the importance of preparing for potential scenarios using the analogy of a fire drill. By conducting a hypothetical fire drill and thoroughly examining their agreements, they may begin to feel uneasy and question whether their agreement falls within the 90% with significant flaws. This story about fire drills has proven highly effective in raising awareness among both professionals and clients.

The reality is that poorly drafted or ambiguous buy/sell agreements often result in litigation. In such cases, it's important to note that in litigation, only the lawyers tend to benefit, as they can defend clients until their resources are depleted.

How can people learn more?

Paul Hood: To learn more, people can visit my website at www.paulhoodservices.com. On the website, there are various podcasts, articles, and other informative content under the Resources tab. I have articles that cover topics such as the psychology of estate planning, the human side of estate planning, buy/sell agreements, and more. It's a valuable resource where individuals can find a wealth of information to expand their knowledge.:

About L. Paul Hood, Jr., JD, LL.M.

Author. Speaker. Advisor

L. Paul Hood obtained his undergraduate and law degrees from Louisiana State University and an LL.M. in taxation from Georgetown University Law Center. Paul has taught at the University of New Orleans, Northeastern University, The University of Toledo College of Law and Ohio Northern University Pettit College of Law. Paul has authored or co-authored nine books and over 500 professional articles on estate and tax planning and business valuation. A frequent contributor to Leimberg Information Services since its inception, Paul is a highly sought-after speaker and consultant due to his innate ability to see through complexities and explain complex and even boring subjects in understandable and entertaining language. He minces no words in doing so. Along the way, Paul's been a father, husband, lawyer, trustee, director, president, partner, trust protector, director of planned giving, expert witness, agent, professor, judge, juror, and defendant, and he uses his experience in these myriad roles to guide others.

WEBSITE
https://PaulHoodServices.com

Mastering Leadership and Fulfillment

Donovan Manley is an experienced executive and performance coach who delves into the realm of achieving professional success while finding personal fulfillment. Donovan shares his expertise in helping executives and small business owners elevate their performance, balance their work and personal life, and align their leadership style with their values and future vision. Through thought-provoking questions, guidance, and a comprehensive approach encompassing mindset, behaviors, and capabilities, Donovan empowers his clients to excel as leaders and find fulfillment in their achievements. Join us as we explore the misconceptions about coaching, the benefits of seeking help, and the transformative outcomes that can be achieved through a holistic coaching journey.

Conversation with Donovan Manley

Who do you help, and how do you assist them?

Donovan Manley: I primarily assist executives and small business owners —leaders—seeking to enhance their performance and find greater fulfillment. The relentless pursuit of success in business can often lead to neglecting personal growth and sacrificing work-life balance. My objective is to guide these individuals in aligning these aspects by creating a vision of a harmonious work-life balance. I provide support in not only excelling professionally but also deriving satisfaction from their achievements while enjoying a well-rounded life beyond work. Through coaching, I help them take the necessary steps to achieve this desired equilibrium.

What is the primary problem your clients seek help in solving?

Donovan Manley: When clients approach me, they have already achieved a certain level of success but often question whether there is more to it. They wonder if they have to continue grinding relentlessly to reach the next level or maintain success, and if so, how they can find enjoyment in that process. There is often a dilemma of whether they have to delay their fulfillment until retirement to truly succeed at what they do.

In my experience, I've found that by aligning their leadership style with their values and future vision, they not only become better leaders but also find greater balance and harmony in their lives. This is usually the starting point of our conversations. Many individuals come to me with specific goals, but we dive a bit deeper, and they realize they need a personal development plan. There's this perception that once they reach a certain level, they are left to figure things out on their own. Unlike in the military, where promotions are based on potential and development activities are provided, the civilian community often lacks a structured development process for senior leaders. After promotion, individuals are expected to possess the necessary skills for their new role. This is where my assistance becomes valuable.

Some clients seek a sounding board to discuss ideas and goals with and help them navigate the mindset, behaviors, and skills required to reach the next level or achieve their objectives without burning out. Through our conversations, they realize that they have been dedicating everything to their job while neglecting their own needs. It may seem selfish, but in reality, it makes them better leaders for their teams when they can confidently say, "I am fulfilled in what I do. I am skilled, and I genuinely enjoy my work."

How do you help clients improve their performance?

Donovan Manley: To enhance performance, I take a comprehensive approach that considers mindset, behaviors, and capabilities, tailoring it to each individual's specific needs. It all starts with cultivating the right mindset. I help clients clarify their goals, understand their strengths, and align with their values. With this foundation, we work on implementing behaviors and establishing routines that support their growth. Developing the necessary capabilities and skills for their roles is crucial, so I focus on enhancing their leadership competencies.

One of my strengths is the ability to address all three aspects—mindset, behaviors, and capabilities—due to my experience, education, and credentials. I believe in the interconnectedness of these areas and avoid solely focusing on one while neglecting the others. Well-being also plays a significant role in my approach. Having served as a paratrooper, I understand the importance of physical fitness for leaders. Consequently, I obtained certifications as a master fitness trainer and nutrition coach. We can address health-related aspects such as stress management, sleep, nutrition, and activity levels if needed. However, the key is to tailor the approach to enhance each client's performance and overall well-being.

What is the greatest benefit or advantage that clients gain from working with you?

Donovan Manley: The most significant benefit or advantage clients receive from working with me is the comprehensive combination of mindset, behaviors, and skills. We focus on enhancing their leadership skills, communication, time management, delegation, and other areas that contribute to their professional growth. Simultaneously, I guide clients in cultivating a positive mindset, clarifying their goals, overcoming obstacles and limiting beliefs, and creating a path forward. We also work on developing empowering behaviors and establishing daily routines that support their progress.

The key advantage of working with me lies in the holistic approach I provide. Clients not only receive guidance on what may be holding them back but also gain valuable insight and support to propel them forward. This approach ensures that their journey encompasses not just performance improvement but also overall well-being and fulfillment. By addressing these interconnected aspects, clients undergo transformative and comprehensive growth that positively impacts both their professional and personal lives.

Do clients often have misconceptions about your role?

Donovan Manley: Yes, it is common for clients to have misconceptions about the role of a coach compared to that of a consultant or trainer. When organizations bring in a leadership trainer or consultant, they expect them to teach specific concepts and provide ready-made solutions for implementation. However, as a coach, my approach is different. My role is to facilitate clients in finding their own answers. I help them uncover their strengths, explore their plans, ask thought-provoking questions, challenge assumptions, and encourage them to think differently about their goals. While I possess knowledge and resources, I believe that clients often hold the answers within themselves, and my job is to guide them toward discovering and taking ownership of their solutions. Together, we focus on action steps and accountability, considering how they can progress and what steps to take next. It is about helping clients tap into their own wisdom and empowering them to actively participate in designing their solutions.

Another misconception arises from the belief that once someone reaches a certain level, they should have all the answers and not require assistance. Clients may feel guilty or hesitant about seeking help because they think they should already know everything about leadership. The truth is, nobody knows everything. Even with 30 years of experience, I continue to learn every day. Clients need to understand that seeking support and guidance does not diminish their capabilities but rather enhances their growth as leaders.

What prevents people from seeking the help you offer?

Donovan Manley: One of the main obstacles is the fear of vulnerability. It is natural for individuals to hesitate when seeking help and sharing their doubts with someone else. In certain environments, like the military, expressing doubts during planning sessions is encouraged as it drives you to gather crucial information for informed decision-making. However, in some professional settings, there can be an expectation that leaders should have all the answers, and the leader may feel that admitting uncertainty will be perceived as a sign of incompetence. Overcoming this mindset and realizing that it is perfectly acceptable to seek assistance and ask questions is essential.

Having an executive or performance coach provides the benefit of a safe space where individuals can express their doubts without judgment or concern about their reputation. Clients who work with a coach become more comfortable acknowledging their uncertainties and understanding the critical information they need to make sound decisions. Gradually, some clients gain the confidence to bring those questions and doubts to their boards or C-suite, recognizing the importance of gathering the necessary information for making quality decisions. In the short term, I serve as a sounding board, helping clients work through their assumptions and identify the answers they need to make informed choices.

The initial clarity sessions focus on helping potential clients gain a clear vision of what they truly want. It's not just about attaching numbers or specific outcomes but about deeply understanding how their life would look if they were aligned with their values, operating within their strengths, and making meaningful contributions. This vision becomes a decision filter, guiding them in assessing whether a particular choice brings them closer to their vision and aligns with their values. If the answer is yes, they pursue it; if it's no, it becomes an easy decision to let go. These conversations help individuals gain clarity; for some, that clarity is all they need. They leave with a renewed sense of direction and can check back in later if they require further support. Others may delve deeper, exploring their character strengths and developing personalized strategies for personal growth and development, and that's where our work continues.

Can you provide an example of an outcome resulting from your coaching?

Donovan Manley: Certainly! Let me share an example that illustrates the impact of our work together. I once had a client who was an engineer with exceptional technical expertise. They had steadily progressed through supervisory and management roles and were being considered for a general manager position. However, they began feeling uncertain and uncomfortable as they transitioned into higher-level leadership roles. They doubted whether they had what it takes to excel in a broader leadership capacity. At that point, their mentor recommended they seek my assistance, and we started our coaching engagement.

During our coaching sessions, we focused on developing their leadership perspective. We examined leaders they admired and analyzed their approaches to their roles. We explored the qualities and behaviors they aspired to embody as a leader. Through our discussions, the client discovered they already possessed many of the necessary leadership skills; they simply hadn't recognized them as such. They had been viewing their abilities solely within the context of managing projects, delivering results, and coordinating teams. However, by reframing their experiences, they realized that these were all manifestations of leadership skills in action. They learned to translate their technical expertise into leadership language and appreciate the broader impact of their work.

As a direct result of our coaching, the client experienced a significant shift in their confidence and work-life balance. They felt more at ease pursuing the general manager role and became more effective in their current position. They no longer felt the need to overwork to prove themselves. Instead, they found ways to leverage their strengths and talents, increasing efficiency and effectiveness. Moreover, they were able to enjoy a more fulfilling personal life, spending quality time with their family and pursuing leisure activities like visiting their beach house in the summers or attending their children's baseball games. This example demonstrates that moving to a higher leadership level does not necessarily require sacrificing work-life balance. With the right strategies and mindset, it is possible to achieve both professional success and personal fulfillment.

In this particular case, the decision to seek coaching was not solely the client's own but rather a recommendation from their mentor. However, it underscores the overall impact of working with a coach. Through a holistic approach, we identify individual strengths, help individuals leverage them effectively, and enhance their overall effectiveness and enjoyment of their work.

How did you get started in this field?

Donovan Manley: After retiring from the military, I took management roles in manufacturing and then at a health club. When I decided to do something on my own, I realized that I missed being involved in leadership development the way we had focused on it in the military. I have always found great fulfillment in helping others grow and become more effective leaders.

During this time, I began discussing my passion for leadership development with my network, and people expressed interest in receiving coaching from me. I started coaching individuals on a freelance basis, utilizing my tools and credentials to provide guidance. As I immersed myself more deeply into coaching, I recognized that this was a path I wanted to pursue full-time. I established my own company and expanded my reach to corporate clients on a larger scale while still focusing on my core mission—using my nearly 30 years of experience in leadership development and well-being to help individuals feel fulfilled in their work and enhance their performance.

It has been an incredibly rewarding journey, combining my love for leadership development with the opportunity to support others in achieving their goals and finding greater satisfaction in their professional lives.

What criteria should people use when evaluating potential help?

Donovan Manley: When evaluating potential help, it is important to start by determining exactly what you are seeking.

Do you need a consultant to assess your business and provide implementation recommendations? Or are you looking for a coach to help you evaluate your current situation and help you develop an action plan with resources and tools to support your progress? You can find the right fit once you have clarity on the assistance you require.

Consider the specific area of focus that you need help with. Is it leadership development, health, and well-being, or strategic planning for your company? Different coaching companies and coaches specialize in various areas, so seek out those who align with your needs.

Another important aspect to consider is whether the coach primarily provides a process to follow or asks questions to find the right process for you. This can be a deciding factor because if you are forced into a rigid framework that doesn't suit your needs, you may not achieve the desired outcome. While every coach has some framework or structure, it should be adaptable and tailored to your unique situation and goals.

Chemistry and rapport with the coach are vital. Effective coaching requires a personal connection, often involving deep discussions, introspection, and sharing. It is essential to have trust and comfort with the coach, knowing that they understand your circumstances and can guide you effectively. People have different preferences and may connect better with certain coaches, even if they possess similar credentials. Therefore, it is advisable to have chemistry meetings or calls with two or three potential coaches before deciding to engage with one.

By considering these criteria—understanding your specific needs, the coach's approach, and the chemistry between you and the coach—you can make an informed choice that aligns with your goals and ensures a productive coaching relationship.

How can people find more information?

Donovan Manley: To learn more, the best way is to visit my website at stalwartperformance.com. You can also connect with me on LinkedIn, where I am active as Donovan Manley. If you have any questions or want further information, please don't hesitate to reach out through the website or LinkedIn. I'll gladly provide you with additional details and address any inquiries.

Donovan Manley

Donovan Manley is a retired Infantry Officer and Paratrooper. He applies nearly three decades of leadership, development, and coaching experience to help his clients be all they can be under even the most stressful conditions.

WEBSITE
https://StalwartPerformance.com

Streamlining Operations
in Mid-Market Companies

Lynda Roth is a professional known for assisting mid-market companies in leveraging technology to thrive in the 21st-century economy. Lynda sheds light on the challenges companies face when determining their information technology needs and integrating suitable systems. She emphasizes the importance of streamlining operations through technology and fostering interconnectivity with customers and suppliers.

Lynda dispels common myths surrounding the availability and affordability of technology solutions. With her extensive background in small and mid-sized businesses, she brings a unique perspective to the table, offering insights into the criteria for evaluating back-office systems and highlighting the pitfalls to avoid during implementation. Through her guidance, Lynda empowers mid-market companies to become digitally driven, interconnected businesses poised for success in the modern era.

Conversation with Lynda Roth

What types of companies do you work with, and how do you assist them?

Lynda Roth: I primarily work with mid-market companies, typically ranging from $50 million to $1 billion in revenue. Some of these businesses have surpassed the billion-dollar mark, while others are smaller, such as the marketing company I'm assisting with revenue of just under $40 million. Despite the range, these companies often struggle to determine their information technology needs and integrate them effectively.

In a recent client engagement, the owner expressed the desire for new systems but had budget constraints that limited their options. However, I assured them that suitable solutions were available. My role was to help them identify the right technologies and guide them through the implementation process.

My main objective is to assist these companies in transforming into 21st-century businesses by leveraging technology. Regardless of the industry they belong to, embracing digital operations is essential for their profitability and growth. I often refer to it as "surviving and thriving in the 21st-century economy." To illustrate this, I draw parallels with the transformative technological advancements of the 19th and early 20th centuries, such as the telephone, electricity, and the light bulb, which revolutionized industries. During that time, small shops and craftsmen gave way to large companies that eventually became industry giants.

Similarly, in the 21st century, digital technologies emerged in the 1990s. Initially, businesses primarily used them internally for tasks like accounting. The Internet has revolutionized the landscape of business operations, enabling companies to connect and interact in unprecedented ways, and it is surprising how many are still operating with outdated technology and not taking advantage of cloud-based systems to work more efficiently.

Returning to the example of my client in the food and nutraceutical chemicals industry, their core production remains the same. However, instead of relying on spreadsheets and manual processes to manage production schedules and cust-omer interactions, they can now leverage advanced technology to become an interconnected and streamlined enterprise.

How do you assist them in streamlining their operations using technology?

Lynda Roth: My role involves helping businesses streamline operations using technology to enhance communication with suppliers and customers. Take the procurement process, for instance. Traditionally, companies have dedicated procure-ment departments that handle tasks like purchase orders and supplier selection using manual processes. However, these tasks can now be streamlined through digital means.

I recall a case where a potential client, who manufactured small dishes for frozen food dinners, initially dismissed my suggestions as impractical. He expressed frustration with receiving frequent rush orders from the food companies he supplied. I explained to him that his inventory, which consisted of the products provided to the food manufacturers, was considered a "C level" inventory. This meant that the manufacturers didn't regularly monitor it, leading to last-minute rush orders when they realized they lacked specific dishes needed for their food products.

I proposed integrating his business with the food manufacturers' enterprise resource planning (ERP) systems to address this challenge. By connecting with their ERP systems, he would gain visibility into their manufacturing schedules, enabling him to anticipate their needs and proactively produce the required dishes aligned with their production plans.

What are the main challenges companies face when researching new systems?

Lynda Roth: When researching new systems, many mid-market companies encounter significant challenges. The executives and owners of these companies understand the importance of upgrading their systems. Still, they often struggle with the high costs associated with well-known brands like Oracle, SAP, or Microsoft Dynamics, which dominate the market. This creates a dilemma because software companies targeting the mid-market segment face difficulties gaining visibility and recognition compared to larger vendors.

One of my key roles is presenting alternative options to help these companies save money on software systems. This involves reducing immediate costs and considering the long-term expenses associated with system upgrades and digital transformation.

I remember working with a metal distributor in California that faced a similar situation. Despite generating significant revenue, they were still using an outdated 1980s system. Their small IT department focused primarily on day-to-day operations and lacked the knowledge of the company's actual system needs and where to find appropriate solutions. When CEOs and decision-makers in such situations start researching new systems, they often encounter an overwhelming amount of information about expensive options like Oracle, SAP, and Microsoft Dynamics. The price tags associated with these systems often reach tens of millions, leading companies to believe that no other viable alternatives are available.

However, a market segment of mid-market systems offers suitable solutions. It surprises me that these mid-market systems have not invested more in promoting their offerings to increase awareness. Nevertheless, my career revolves around familiarizing myself with these systems, building relationships with reliable vendors, and connecting them with companies that express the need for systems but have concerns about affordability. Unlike large consulting firms, I offer a distinct advantage by presenting alternatives beyond the big-name software systems often recommended by major accounting or consulting firms.

How do you assist companies in overcoming challenges during the implementation of more efficient systems?

Lynda Roth: To help companies implement more efficient systems, one crucial aspect is emphasizing the significance of interconnectivity with their customers and suppliers. I explain the value of integrating with their customers' ERP systems, which grants visibility into manufacturing schedules. This enables proactive preparation and readiness for orders, eliminating the need for last-minute rush orders. However, smaller manufacturers often face challenges when their products constitute only a small part of a larger organization's production needs. The larger organization may not always consider the manufacturing and shipping requirements of the smaller manufacturer.

In today's digital age, manual processes like clerks filling out online forms, printing them, or sending them via email are unnecessary. Instead, we focus on implementing systems that facilitate seamless information flow. For example, in the case of the food manufacturer and the company producing small dishes, integration plays a vital role. The smaller dish-making company can establish integration with the food manufacturer's ERP system, receiving notifications when orders are placed. This integration process requires careful planning and assistance, which is where I step in to help identify suitable solutions and integration providers.

It's important to clarify that when I mention "manual" processes, I refer to individuals still having to input information by typing on a computer. While physical paper usage may be eliminated, the essence of manual processes remains. Therefore, transitioning from physical mail to email represents a significant step towards digitization and streamlining operations.

What are some common myths and misconceptions about your work?

Lynda Roth: There are a couple of prevalent myths and misconceptions surrounding my work with mid-market companies. Firstly, many company executives and owners are often unaware of the available technology solutions and how to find them. They may believe that only large, well-known software brands are viable options, unaware of the mid-market systems that can effectively meet their needs at a more affordable cost.

Secondly, there is a misconception about the partnership between mid-market companies and larger corporations like Walmart and Amazon. These retail giants collaborate with numerous small manufacturers that supply products for their shelves. However, these companies have strict processes and requirements that must be followed for inventory to be stocked in their stores. Walmart, for example, has implemented automated processes to manage its supply chain. If a smaller business is not integrated into Walmart's automated process, its inventory will not make it onto Walmart's shelves.

In my perspective, being a 21st-century business means being interconnected, establishing seamless communication and collaboration with customers and suppliers. This interconnectedness is crucial for companies to thrive in the digital age and remain competitive.

What are some common mistakes mid-market companies make when integrating their business systems?

Lynda Roth: Mid-market companies often make several common mistakes when integrating their business systems. Firstly, some companies tend to give up too easily, assuming that no suitable solutions are available for their needs. This misconception can hinder their progress in finding the right system to streamline their operations effectively.

Secondly, some companies make the mistake of choosing larger, complex systems that are not a good fit for their organization. These systems often come with high costs, not only in terms of the initial investment but also in ongoing expenses. Working with big consulting firms can further escalate costs, as they often charge high hourly rates for consultants who may not fully grasp the intricacies and specific requirements of mid-market businesses.

Additionally, when larger consulting firms send junior staff to mid-market companies, there can be a disconnect between their theoretical knowledge and the practical realities of running a business. These junior consultants may approach the integration process with a one-size-fits-all mentality, relying solely on frameworks learned in their MBA programs.

However, this approach may not align with the unique needs and operations of mid-market companies.

I bring a valuable perspective as someone with a small business background. Growing up, my father owned an HVAC system company, and I gained hands-on experience working in the office from a young age. This firsthand experience has given me insights into the workings of small and mid-sized businesses. Although I have also worked in larger corporations such as Ralston Purina and Levi Strauss, I understand the specific needs and challenges mid-market companies face.

What are the key criteria for corporations to evaluate back-office systems to improve operations?

Lynda Roth: When evaluating back-office systems to improve operations, corporations should consider several criteria. First and foremost, the system should be built on an open architecture platform, allowing for easy integration with other systems within the company. This means it should not be a closed platform that restricts connectivity and interoperability.

An effective back-office system should be browser-based, utilizing internet capabilities and programming languages that enable seamless integration. This facilitates efficient communication and data sharing between systems, promoting connectivity with customers and suppliers. The focus should be on being an interconnected business, where systems can communicate without manual interventions such as sending emails or relying on spreadsheets.

Assessing the system's ability to streamline processes, automate tasks, and enhance overall operational efficiency is crucial. The system should support essential functionalities such as financial management, procurement, inventory management, reporting, and analytics. It should also offer scalability to accommodate business growth and adapt to changing needs over time.

Integration capabilities, user-friendly interfaces, data security measures, and robust support and maintenance services should be considered during the evaluation process. The system should align with the specific requirements and objectives of the corporation, providing a comprehensive and flexible solution that enhances operational effectiveness.

How can we find more information about you?

Lynda Roth: To find more information about me and my work, you can visit my website at ljrcs.com. The website provides comprehensive details about my background and the services LJR Consulting Services offers.

If you prefer direct communication, you can call me at 818-216-7264. I'm always available to answer calls and provide assistance. Alternatively, you can email me at lynda@ljrcs.com for any inquiries or further communication.

Please feel free to explore my website or contact me directly for more information or if you have any specific questions.

WEBSITE
http://ljrcs.com/

About Lynda J. Roth

Lynda J. RothLynda Roth is an Information Technology pioneer with a career that has spanned the decades from mainframes to client-servers to digital technologies. Lynda spent 25 years transforming organizations as a Senior Technology Executive and Digital Economy Strategist. She guides companies through transformations using digital technology to remain relevant in the 21st-century economy, create a competitive advantage, accelerate business growth, and increase customer reach.

Lynda's interest in business began working in the family HVAC business at a young age. She started her career as a software developer in Fortune 500 companies, leading her to IT management. She established her first technical consulting practice working with enterprises to implement financial, manufacturing, and CRM applications. While these systems advanced corporate transaction processing, they left an information void for management. That observation inspired Lynda to launch a software/consulting firm. She and her partners developed a business intelligence application to support executive decision-making.

During the early years of her career, her clients included Ralston Purina, Levi Strauss & Co., McDonnell Douglas Aerospace & Defense, American Medical International, First Interstate Bank, Saks Fifth Avenue, Shearson Lehman Hutton, American Express Bank, Glendale Federal Bank, Aramark Uniform Services and Mattel Toy Company.

Later Lynda founded LJR Consulting Services to advise clients on the digital transformations they must make to attain their strategic and operational goals. She has a unique capability to work with owners, management, and team members to identify critical business challenges resulting from the massive business and societal shift in the digital economy. She then successfully and economically delivers these solutions so her client companies will create significant long-term competitive advantages. She has led teams to transform traditional businesses to remain relevant and increase corporate value in the digital economy.

Lynda is the author of "Digital Transformation – An Executive Guide to Survive and Thrive in the New Economy." She is also the past president and member of the Board of Directors of ACG101 (Association for Corporate Growth Ventura Chapter) and past Chair of the San Fernando Valley Chapter of the Institute of Management Consultants in Southern California.

Strategic Property Management (SPM)

Strategic Property Management (SPM) believes that you need the best people in the industry to provide the best service. Becoming the best takes time, energy, effort, and an unrelenting desire to improve consistently.

SPM has put together a winning team. Through their efforts and collaboration with their clients, they consistently provide outstanding results.

With a unique combination of personalities, styles, strengths, passions, and experience, SPM is here to serve you.

Conversation with Jaime Sepulveda

Were there any signs or clues that you had the entrepreneurial gene in your DNA?

Jaime Sepulveda: I remember when my grandmother made flour tortillas to sell. I was probably two or three years old, and I couldn't even reach the top of the table where she stacked the tortillas. I remember just trying to reach up and grab one to eat. My grandma and I would ride the bus to deliver the tortillas, and I always looked forward to getting a toy after we finished our route.

In fourth grade, I noticed that kids were going to the ice cream truck after school and buying Salt Lucas, a Mexican candy. I couldn't understand why they were getting so excited about it when it was something we had in our pantry at home. I saw an opportunity to sell the candy at school, so I put some in my backpack and sold it for a nickel, a dime, or 50 cents. I probably cleaned out my parents' pantry in just a day or two!

I had to confess to my parents, but my dad was supportive and gave me a bag of candy to sell. They sold like crazy, and I would come home with a bag full of change to buy Nintendo games and Legos. This is when I first saw the potential of entrepreneurship. My dad also had an entrepreneurial mindset and started his own business, which inspired me to keep going.

I've never worked for corporate America and have always done my own thing. My dad's support was crucial to my success, and I'm grateful. Many of us go into entrepreneurship because we see the potential and have supportive people around us. While paying attention in school is important, I'm glad my dad supported me even though I wasn't the brightest student.

What kind of student were you?

Jaime Sepulveda: I used to think life would be easier if I were a great student. I wasn't terrible, but I was more of a C or D+ student. I didn't love being in school and often thought about what activities I could do instead. I was always excited about PE or gym class, playing basketball or baseball, or running around with friends.

I discovered organized sports in seventh grade when I joined the football team. I was so excited, but then I learned I needed good grades to stay on the team. I was discouraged at first, but then I noticed my grades were improving. As I moved on to high school, I focused more on basketball. I really enjoyed it, but my coaches always stressed the importance of grades. I found that I did better in school when I had a clear goal, like staying on the basketball team.

I've heard from many entrepreneurs that they were average or below-average students. They only did well in subjects that interested them. This doesn't mean they weren't intelligent, just that they were more motivated by their interests. There are many ways to be intelligent, but the school system often only recognizes one type.

My dad recognized that I was motivated by things outside of school and supported me in pursuing those interests. As parents, we should look for ways to support our children's unique interests and talents, even if they don't fit into the traditional school system.

What inspired you to decide that you were going to become a business owner?

Jaime Sepulveda: I never really worked in a corporate job. During high school, I sold things to make some money. My dad started a business, and I also helped him for a few years. Around the early 2000s, I started renovating properties and got into real estate. My dad and I were starting to phase out our business then, so I had to decide what to do next. I really enjoyed the real estate side of things, so I decided to get licensed in 2006 and see where it would take me. I began exploring different areas of real estate, from brokerage to apartment locating, renovations, and property management. And from there, my career in real estate continued to grow.

Tell me about the moment you created Strategic Property Management.

Jaime Sepulveda: In 2007 and 2008, I had a chance to buy out my broker's business partner to get into the traditional real estate brokerage model. From that point, I started recruiting and training real estate agents. Our goal was to have the best educated and certified real estate agents. We focused on training and certification for about four years, until 2010 and 2011. I received a call from one of our agents with a contract question. Although I was happy to help, I was frustrated with agents who never showed up to training or got certified, yet they took up the most time.

I realized that training and recruiting weren't my specialty. I spoke the investor lingo more naturally, so I started building a small group of investors with around 40 to 50 properties. While I was recruiting agents for four years, I had the opportunity to help my investors acquire investment properties. Eventually, I started to manage their properties, which led me to put in the right systems, processes, and people. In 2011, SPM was born.

What I love about what we do in real estate is that there are so many facets to it. We have the chance to help investors and clients, as well as tenants and residents. When we all work together, we can create a great product. This means that residents have a beautiful home to make memories in, and investors have an investment that performs very well. We can help these individuals move in the right direction.

What was the reaction from friends and family about your decision?

Jaime Sepulveda: Starting a business was made possible by the unwavering support of my parents. They have always been there for me, providing encouragement and guidance as I navigate the challenges of entrepreneurship. When I first started, I was not yet married, which made things a little easier to manage as a single person. However, when I met my now-wife during the early stages of building my business, she was incredibly supportive.

Entrepreneurship is not for the faint of heart. There were countless sleepless nights and times when my checking account was nearly empty. Issues would arise, and it was easy to become discouraged. But my parents, family, and spouse never lost faith in me. They were my biggest fans, cheering me on every step of the way. I am certain that I could not have achieved what I have without their unwavering support.

In today's world, it is rare to find such a strong support system. Many people are quick to discourage, even if they have good intentions. Parents, for example, may worry about the uncertainty of entrepreneurship and the risks involved. But if you are lucky enough to find people who believe in you and support your dreams, it can make all the difference. Having that kind of support is a rarity, but it is also essential to success.

Have you experienced any failures that you now realize directly contributed to the success you have today?

Jaime Sepulveda: As an entrepreneur who has been in the game for a couple of decades, I have learned that failures are inevitable. Even when you reach a level of success, there will still be failures along the way. In fact, I have come to expect failures and even use them as a tool and resource. Being comfortable with failure is necessary to being a successful entrepreneur because you have to go through them to find the lessons that will help you in your next venture.

I have experienced more failures than successes but have learned to become comfortable with them. From a 30,000-foot view, there are many aspects to consider as an entrepreneur, such as business partnerships. I once had a business partner that seemed perfect from the beginning, but eventually, our relationship deteriorated due to a difference in opinion on how much effort should be given to the business. Looking back, I realize that we held onto the partnership for too long, which negatively impacted our business.

I have come to accept that no one has a crystal ball, and we can never predict what lies ahead. Instead of dwelling on negative experiences, I choose to focus on the present and future opportunities. Even though that partnership was tough for me at a younger age, I have learned from it and taken it as a lesson for the future. I may face similar challenges in the future, but I will take different steps to protect myself better.

What's it like being the Jaime Sepulveda you are today?

Jaime Sepulveda: Today, in strategic property management, I believe that building relationships and having support is the key to success. I'm so grateful to have an amazing team that does the heavy lifting. Without them, our tenants, clients, and vendors would not have the experiences they have today. They have the opportunity to grow their investment portfolios, make memories in their homes or communities, and build their families or businesses. We help residential real estate investors find investment properties and manage them. This means we take care of everything from HOA dues or situations to rents, maintenance, renovations, and even the occasional eviction. If we have to do an eviction, we also take care of all the legal aspects.

We help our investor clients achieve their goals, just like entrepreneurs. They may have different mindsets and backgrounds, but they understand the benefits of real estate in their future. We manage their portfolios so that they can retire in 20 years, use it for their kids' college funds, or buy their forever home once they retire. Everyone has different reasons, and we are grateful to be part of their lives and help them achieve their dreams.

I strongly believe in building relationships and working as a team. You can't do everything yourself, and working together is much more enriching. As I learned from experience, it's impossible to do everything alone. It's much better to do it as a team, as a community, and to help others build something they will enjoy in the future. As a team at SPM, we strive to help individuals build something they will flourish in for years.

How do you recharge from business, and who do you spend your non-business time with?

Jaime Sepulveda: I have come to appreciate the value of balancing my life as an entrepreneur. It can be tempting to keep pushing myself nonstop, but there are more important things in life. For me, family comes first. I have an eight-year-old son who is at a great age for exploring new activities and sports and spending time with him is a priority for me outside of work.

In addition to my family, I also enjoy doing community work. I volunteer with several non-profit organizations that focus on helping underprivileged children. These activities take up a lot of my time, but I find them rewarding and fulfilling. Between work, family, and community work, I stay pretty busy. But I know we all have the same 24 hours in a day, and it's up to us to make the most of them.

Living in this amazing country has allowed me to pursue my passions and goals. It's never easy to achieve success, and there's no easy route. But I believe that if you work hard and stay committed to your dreams, you can achieve anything you want.

How can we learn more about Jaime Sepulveda and continue following the journey?

Jaime Sepulveda: My webpage is spm-roi.com, and you can easily locate it online. If you want to contact me, you can call me directly at (210) 672-4000 or reach out to me on social media platforms. I must admit that social media is not my forte, so we are currently outsourcing that part.

About Jaime Sepulveda

Before co-founding Strategic Property Management in 2006, Jaime operated a successful exporting company for over a decade. The experience of being an entrepreneur constantly reminds him of the importance of delivering a return on investment. During those early years, he learned the importance of creating the right return on investment for himself and his investing partners.

With Jaime's strong principles built on trust and honesty, he understands the importance of having the right information available to his clients. This helps clients know that the correct decisions are being made, resulting in a high level of trust and leading to long-lasting relationships. He puts his client's needs first, allowing him to focus on building a very successful referral-based business that he now can expand on through the dominant team Strategic Property Management has assembled.

LOCATION
9901 IH-10 W Suite 800, San Antonio, Texas 78230

WEBSITE
https://spm-roi.com/

PHONE
+1 210.672.4000

EMAIL
jsepulveda@spm-roi.com

Achieving Financial Balance
for Entrepreneurs

Shannon Simmons is the founder of Fit for Profit, a coaching and bookkeeping service specializing in helping those in the fitness and wellness industry. Shannon addresses the common challenges faced by business owners in determining their salaries, emphasizing the importance of striking a balance between business growth and personal income. She highlights the misconceptions surrounding reinvesting all profits back into the business and the need for effective communication and collaboration with bookkeepers.

Shannon also shares a success story that showcases how her solution enabled a client to pay herself during maternity leave, demonstrating the tangible benefits of the Profit First methodology.

Conversation with Shannon Simmons

What is Fit for Profit, and who do you assist?

Shannon Simmons: Fit for Profit is a coaching and bookkeeping service that primarily supports business owners in the fitness and wellness industry. Our goal is to help them effectively manage their cash flow and ensure they have tangible profits in their bank accounts. We want them to experience real financial growth instead of just seeing positive numbers on their profit and loss statements that don't translate into actual cash that supports a better lifestyle for the business owner.

What challenges do business owners face when it comes to paying themselves?

Determining the appropriate amount to pay themselves is a common struggle for many business owners. It's not as simple as writing a check or transferring money to their personal accounts, which many do early in business. The challenge lies in having consistent funds in the business to pay themselves and maintain the desired lifestyle their business should provide. Essentially, it's about taking a regular paycheck from their business for the hard work they put into it.

Why do business owners often struggle with determining their salary?

Shannon Simmons: Many business owners, including myself as an accountant, face this challenge because we typically lack formal education in business management. We excel in our specific fields but aren't prepared for the financial aspects of running a business.

Additionally, our decision-making is influenced by psychological factors, such as Parkinson's Law. This phenomenon suggests that we tend to consume all the resources available to us. When it comes to finances, if we have a certain amount in our bank account to run our business, we often spend the entire sum on business-related expenses (whether they're necessary expenses or not) without considering our own compensation.

As business owners, we're also prone to distractions and expenses that seem necessary for business growth. Things like new equipment, attending conferences, and shiny marketing tactics seem like something we "need," and we prioritize these expenses over paying ourselves. This leads to a lack of personal funds.

To address this, our approach at Fit for Profit focuses on paying yourself first and establishing a structure that ensures your personal income is taken care of before other expenses. By creating and using multiple bank accounts, we can compartmentalize funds for profit, owner compensation, and tax savings, ensuring separate allocations for each purpose.

Our goal is to simplify cash flow management and alleviate the psychological and mindset aspects associated with it. Using an automated system with pre-determined allocations for each bank account, we take the guesswork out of business finances. This structure allows for spending from the operating expense account while safeguarding profit, personal income, and tax savings.

What is the main goal your clients hope to achieve through your services?

Shannon Simmons: The main goal our clients strive for is the ability to pay themselves from their businesses. When people start their businesses, their intention is not to end up financially strained, yet it's a common outcome. Therefore, the primary objective is to find a balance where the business has enough funds to operate effectively while also providing the business owner with a personal income that allows them to maintain the lifestyle they want. We aim to help our clients in achieving this balance.

What are the common misconceptions you encounter when people approach you as clients?

Shannon Simmons: Individuals often have a couple of misconceptions before becoming our clients. First, many believe that to grow their business, every dollar must be reinvested back into it. They think they can't take any money out for personal needs until they reach a certain milestone. However, successful companies like Google and Amazon started small and focused on operational efficiency rather than excessive spending. While reinvestment is important, it's not necessary to allocate all funds back into the business. It's possible to pay yourself and earn a personal income while still growing the business.

Another misconception relates to bookkeeping. Some assume they can fully outsource it without any involvement or communication. While bookkeepers handle most of the work independently, business owners need to communicate to their bookkeeper important information about new transactions or specific activities in their business. Bookkeepers rely on this collaboration to ensure accurate and comprehensive financials. Being prepared to engage with your financial professionals and maintain open communication is important.

How do you help clients overcome these fears or misconceptions?

Shannon Simmons: To address the misconception around allocating owner's pay, we introduce clients to the Profit First methodology we follow. When they realize that we recommend putting aside profit and paying themselves a certain percentage of their revenue, they may feel overwhelmed, especially if they have yet to pay themselves anything.

In these situations, we reassure them that implementing new financial systems doesn't require an immediate leap from zero to the recommended percentage. Instead, we encourage them to start small and take incremental steps. We like to start by having them pay themselves a minimal amount every two weeks, regardless of how modest it may be. The key is to initiate the process and establish the habit, even if the initial payment is small. Over time, we work together to improve and increase their compensation. The important thing is to start and gradually build momentum.

Can you provide a specific example of how your solution has benefited a client?

Shannon Simmons: We had a client who wanted to be able to pay herself a salary while on maternity leave. It was important to her to take time off from her business so she could be fully present during the newborn phase. However, she had concerns about managing her finances during this period.

We worked with this client for about six months before she had her baby. During that time, we aligned her percentage allocations to allow her to pay herself her full salary for the first three months of her maternity leave. How great is it that she could be fully present for her child without sacrificing her personal finances? When we began, her business was already operating at a nearly profitable level. Our focus was on further increasing her profitability.

One of the key steps we took was conducting a thorough evaluation of her expenses. We identified areas where we could reduce unnecessary or excessive costs, which allowed her to allocate more funds toward saving for her own compensation during her planned time off. This strategic approach ensured she was financially prepared to step away from her business and embrace motherhood. It's one of my favorite success stories, seeing the positive impact our solution had on her life during such a crucial and special time.

What criteria do you suggest entrepreneurs consider when choosing a bookkeeper?

Shannon Simmons: When selecting a bookkeeper, there are several important criteria to consider. First, finding someone who makes you feel comfortable and who you have good rapport with is crucial. Effective communication is vital, so engaging in conversations with potential bookkeepers via Zoom, email, or phone calls is essential. Your bookkeeper should understand where you're at and be willing to help you build new habits to create new financial systems.

Also, ensure that your bookkeeper uses a reputable online software like QuickBooks Online that allows you and your bookkeeper access at any time.

Another thing to consider when looking for a bookkeeper is the frequency of communication you'll have with them. Establish clear expectations for how often you will meet with your bookkeeper and when. At Fit for Profit, for example, we typically have quarterly meetings with our clients, although this can vary depending on specific business needs. Regular meetings allow for report reviews and discussions about financial matters and questions you might have. Find a bookkeeper who not only has the right expertise to help your business but also acts as a teacher, explaining the meaning of reports for you as a business owner. This educational aspect adds significant value to the services provided.

By considering these criteria—communication, software used, meeting frequency, and the bookkeeper's willingness to educate—you can make an informed decision when selecting a bookkeeper who meets your needs and helps you effectively manage your business finances.

How can individuals find out more information?

To learn more about Fit for Profit, I invite you to visit our website at fitforprofit.com. You can also find us on social media platforms like LinkedIn, Facebook, and Instagram. We have a downloadable overview of our cash flow management system if you're interested. Simply go to fitforprofit.com/trendsetter to access the overview and gain further insights into our approach and how we can assist you in effectively managing your cash flow.

Website: FitForProfit.com

About Shannon Simmons:

Shannon has been consulting with small businesses for more than ten years. After two years in public accounting, she saw a need to work for small business owners to teach them how to grow financially healthy businesses. She has built on her Master of Accountancy degree from Manchester University by becoming a Certified Profit First Professional and a Certified QuickBooks ProAdvisor. When she's not meeting with entrepreneurs or assessing their businesses, she enjoys time with her husband and two children, serving in their community, playing and watching sports, marveling at nature, or reading a good book.

Unveiling the Journey of Holistic Wellness Coaching

Sofiya Stasiv is a licensed professional and lifestyle wellness coach. Sofiya shares her passion for helping individuals reignite the flame for their health and find liberation and joy in their lives through the lens of adventure. Drawing from her background as a nurse, including her experience in kidney and transplant care and as a COVID nurse, Sofiya noticed a gap in post-care resources and the importance of preventive medicine. She focuses on assisting clients who feel lost in their health journey, offering an inside-out approach to bridge the gap between their current state and where they aspire to be. Her emphasis on empowering individuals, addressing mindset obstacles, and fostering a supportive community underscores her dedication to guiding clients on a transformative path toward holistic well-being.

Conversation with Sofiya Stasiv

Who do you help, and how?

Sofiya Stasiv: I assist individuals in their pursuit of reigniting the flame for their health and discovering the accompanying liberation, joy, and adventure. I help those ready to see that health is more than doctor office visits, lab results, or an illness. It is your personal life journey, and it is multifaceted. With my background as a kidney and transplant nurse and my experience as a COVID nurse, I noticed a need for post-care resources in our healthcare system. This led me to focus on clients who are completely adrift regarding their health, sensing that something crucial is missing.

I have always been passionate about preventive medicine, so I primarily work with clients who need guidance in understanding their core identity and adopting an inside-out approach to bridge the gap between their current state and their desired well-being.

What are the benefits of working with you?

Sofiya Stasiv: One of the significant advantages of working with me is that I am a licensed professional with a nursing degree. As a lifestyle wellness coach operating under the nursing specialty of Nurse Coaching, I bring a unique perspective. I prioritize trust, honor, and guiding individuals through their wellness journey. My approach is rooted in a holistic framework, considering various aspects of one's life to foster overall well-being.

My credibility as a nurse enhances the trustworthiness of my services, as nurses are widely recognized as the most trusted professionals in healthcare. I possess a deep understanding of the complex dynamics that influence human life and how they intersect with health. While addressing specific health concerns such as blood pressure or heart rate is important, I also emphasize the significance of establishing boundaries, setting financial standards, and creating an environment that supports overall well-being.

Individuals can embrace a comprehensive circle of self-care by working with me, knowing that my nursing background supports and strengthens my dedication to their well-being.

What outcomes do clients experience when working with you?

Sofiya Stasiv: Working with me often leads to empowering outcomes and increased confidence for my clients. They rediscover their true selves and regain control over their lives. Let me share an example to illustrate this. I had a client who had recently suffered a back injury. Although he had undergone surgery and rehabilitation, he recognized that working with me would provide an opportunity to recalibrate his life. It became apparent that his back injury resulted from being overworked and neglecting proper stress management.

We focused on realigning his values and identifying ways to set more favorable outcomes for himself, both in terms of his desired life trajectory and the pace at which he wanted to achieve it. We also prioritized establishing his future priorities, ensuring he no longer neglected his health.

The outcomes we achieved included a renewed sense of purpose, an improved work-life balance, and a commitment to prioritizing his health. My client gained the empowerment to make choices that aligned with his overall well-being, preventing a recurrence of a similar situation.

What obstacles do your clients face, and how do you help them overcome them?

Sofiya Stasiv: One of the prevalent obstacles I often see among my clients is their mindset, particularly a sense of unworthiness and being haunted by past failures. While they navigate the broader challenges of disease processes and health concerns, it is in our everyday conversations that their self-imposed limitations come to light. There is a recurring theme of striving for perfection, feeling unseen or undeserving of change, and becoming trapped in their own internal world.

I actively collaborate with my clients to address these obstacles, providing them with accountability and support throughout their journey. I am committed to challenging them at every step, encouraging them to break free from their self-perception and limited beliefs about their lives. Moreover, I guide them in rewriting the internal dialogue that shapes their thoughts and behaviors, fostering self-acceptance and facilitating positive change.

It goes beyond improving their eating habits or increasing physical movement; it involves transforming the script within their minds, granting themselves permission, and establishing new empowering patterns. By offering a supportive hand and facilitating a shift in their internal narrative, my clients can overcome these obstacles and embrace a mindset that promotes personal growth, self-worth, and lasting change. They deserve to have their agency back.

What misconceptions exist about your work, and how do you address them?

Sofiya Stasiv: One significant misconception about coaching, particularly in the wellness field, is undervaluing its importance due to a lack of social support in our modern society, which contributes to feelings of loneliness and depression. People must understand that as their coach, I become one of their primary sources of support. However, the impact of coaching goes beyond our interactions; it extends to their environment and the communities they engage with, influenced by the work we do together.

I have witnessed profound transformations in people's lives when they recognize the value of creating a sense of community and connection. Through coaching, individuals can realign their entire lives, finding support and inspiration within their chosen communities. To overcome this misconception, I emphasize the transformative power of community and highlight the ripple effect it can have on overall well-being.

By fostering a sense of connection and demonstrating the significance of building a supportive community, I help my clients understand the immense benefits of embracing coaching as a catalyst for holistic growth and personal development.

What prevents people from seeking the help you offer?

Sofiya Stasiv: One significant barrier I've observed is the absence of quick fixes in the work I do. This can discourage individuals who are seeking immediate solutions. While mindset is a primary focus of my coaching, I often encounter obstacles related to personal investment. Some people may hesitate to invest in themselves due to financial concerns. I accept FSA (Flexible Spending Account) and HSA (Health Savings Account) payments for health-related coaching, but not everyone has a dedicated coaching budget. Additionally, coaching can be overlooked or undervalued, particularly in the healthcare realm, which can further impede affordability.

Furthermore, fear plays a significant role in deterring people from seeking help. Individuals may be apprehensive about taking the risk on themselves and facing their own truths. Engaging in coaching requires vulnerability, authenticity, and honesty, which can be daunting. However, it is precisely in this space that the true beauty of what I do lies, as it allows clients to confront themselves and embark on a transformative journey.

To overcome these barriers, I address financial concerns and emphasize the long-term benefits of investing in oneself. I strive to create a safe and supportive space where clients feel empowered to face their fears, break through limitations, and ultimately experience personal growth and transformation.

How do you help clients overcome those obstacles?

Sofiya Stasiv: To assist clients in overcoming these obstacles, I establish clear agreements during our coaching sessions. These agreements ensure no expectations are placed upon them, creating a safe and supportive environment. I utilize specific coaching tools that foster comfort and encourage open dialogue. I genuinely listen to my clients, engage in therapeutic conversations, and guide them toward recognizing the positive aspects of their experiences rather than solely focusing on the negative.

In many traditional medical settings, individuals often feel judged when they express themselves authentically. However, my approach is different. I encourage clients to embrace their true selves and work together to discover who they aspire to be. We bridge the gap between their current state and their desired future, embarking on a journey of personal growth and self-discovery.

By providing a non-judgmental space where clients can freely express themselves, I help them feel heard and understood. Through our coaching sessions, we collaboratively navigate their obstacles, cultivate resilience, and empower them to make positive changes in their lives.

What inspires you in your work?

Sofiya Stasiv: My inspiration has always come from this idea that adventure is out there in this world. I find so much excitement in the multiple dimensions a human life can be. My personal curiosity about the world and the individuals in it are the inspiration for my coaching. Helping others witness the incredible joy that emanates from within them when they recognize their own worth and the immense potential they have in their lives creates such warmth in my heart. Personally, I have gone through a significant journey of independence, and it can sometimes be a lonely path. While I have been fortunate to have amazing friendships and connections that have supported me, I understand that not everyone has the same privilege.

Having a background in nursing has given me a deep understanding of holistic health and the significance of comprehensive self-care. I genuinely appreciate the importance of taking care of oneself in all aspects of life. However, I also recognize that not everyone has access to such knowledge and resources. This realization, along with my theme of adventure in this life, is a driving force for my inspiration—to bridge the gap and bring everyday wellness practices and storytelling into people's lives.

My ultimate inspiration lies in empowering individuals to embrace their own unique stories and become the main characters in their lives. I am dedicated to creating an environment where people can explore their potential, rewrite their narratives, and embark on a transformative journey toward a happier, healthier, and more fulfilled life. Witnessing the transformative power of personal growth and seeing individuals embrace their true selves fuels my passion and keeps me inspired every single day.

What criteria should people use when evaluating a health and wellness coach?

Sofiya Stasiv: I recommend considering several criteria when evaluating a health and wellness coach. First and foremost, credibility is crucial. It's important to ensure that the coach has the appropriate credentials and qualifications to provide guidance on matters related to your health.

Another important consideration is that the coach operates from a place of heart-centered service. Since coaching conversations can be vulnerable, it's essential to feel comfortable and trust that the coach will create a safe space where you can openly share your thoughts and experiences. They should demonstrate compassion and understanding without judging or ridiculing your decisions. A compassionate and loving coach can acknowledge mistakes while providing support and guidance to facilitate positive changes.

The presence of structure is also important. While each coaching journey is unique, some form of structure should be in place. It's essential to gain clarity on how the coach plans to assist you in achieving your goals. Understanding their methods and approaches ensures that the coaching sessions are productive and purposeful rather than merely casual conversations.

By considering these criteria—credibility, compassion, and structure—you can make an informed decision when selecting a health and wellness coach who aligns with your needs and can provide the necessary support on your wellness journey.

How can we find out more about you and your services?

Sofiya Stasiv: There are several ways to learn more about me and the services I offer. You can visit my personal website at sofiyastasiv.com, where you'll find detailed information about my background, approach, and the services I provide. I offer 1:1 coaching, group coaching, workshops, and retreats. You can also email me at hello@youvsyouwellnesscoaching.com.

I also encourage you to follow me on Instagram (@sofiyastasiv), where I share authentic aspects of my life. Through my posts, I aim to highlight our shared humanity and ongoing growth while offering relatable tips and insights for individuals on their wellness journey.

By exploring my website, following me on Instagram, and considering participating in the upcoming retreat, you can gain a deeper understanding of my services and connect with me personally.

About Sofiya Stasiv

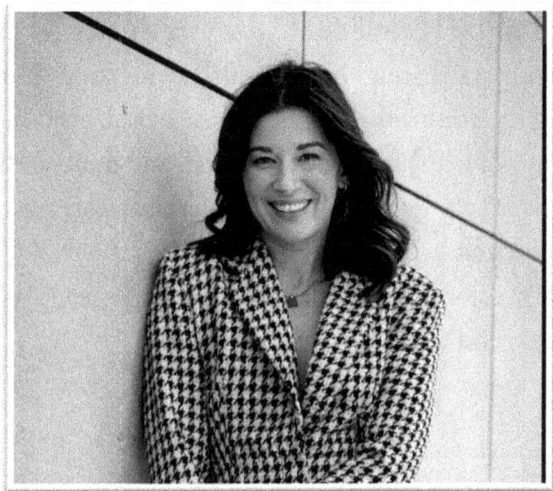

"How you live your life is the influence you have on the world."

Sofiya Stasiv is a Transformational Lifestyle and Wellness Coach and Registered Nurse. She is the founder of You vs You Wellness Coaching. She is a woman full of vibrance, connection, curiosity, and wonder. Her coaching allows others to have an adventurous lens of viewing their health to make sustainable and effective changes.

Sofiya's mission is to help those who have lost sight of their inner flame through the hardships of their pasts by rekindling a bright zest for life once again. She empowers you to stop living in the passenger seat of your life and reclaim it once more through the art of adventuring.

Her story of caring for patients in a conventional medical system from birth until death, deeply investing in the art of connection, navigating being a first-generation immigrant, exploring the cultures and people of the world, and embodying the journey of being your rawest, truest, and honest self has her equipped to help guide you into seeing the world within you and around you in a new lens.

Sofiya's offerings include 1:1 coaching, group coaching, workshops, and retreats."